"Mernissi is one of the most refreshing voices in the emerging feminism of Muslim women."
　　　—*San Francisco Chronicle*

"Fatima Mernissi has more ideas per book than any other thinker in the Middle East. Her later works increasingly integrate her brilliant ideas into sustained and compelling discourse that is very worthy of attention."
　　　—Laurence O. Michalak,
　　　　　Center for Middle Eastern Studies,
　　　　　University of California, Berkeley

"Fatima Mernissi has taken a steady, sustained look into the Muslim heart and emerged with brilliant insights into its fears of the West and of democracy, as well as its love-hate relationship toward its past. She is a psychiatrist of her culture, with understanding for the problems and with courage to move ahead. This is must reading for readers of the West and Middle East alike."
　　　—Arlie Russell Hochschild,
　　　　　Professor of Sociology,
　　　　　University of California, Berkeley
　　　　　Author of *The Second Shift*

"The author of five books on Islam admired for their original and scrupulous research, Mernissi is regarded by many as the pre-eminent Koranic scholar of our time."
　　　—*Vanity Fair*

Islam and Democracy

Other Books by Fatima Mernissi

The Veil and the Male Elite
A Feminist Interpretation of Women's Rights in Islam

Doing Daily Battle
Interviews with Moroccan Women

Beyond the Veil
Male/Female Dynamics in Modern Muslim Society

Islam and Democracy

*Fear of the
Modern World*

FATIMA MERNISSI

TRANSLATED BY
MARY JO LAKELAND

PERSEUS BOOKS

Cambridge, Massachusetts

Library of Congress Cataloging-in-Publication Data

Mernissi, Fatima.
   Islam and democracy : fear of the modern world / Fatima Mernissi ;
translated by Mary Jo Lakeland.
      p. cm.
   Includes index.
   Includes bibliographical references
   ISBN 0-201-60883-9
   ISBN 0-201-62483-4 (pbk.)
   1. Islam—20th century.   2. Civilization, Arab—20th century.
I. Title.
BP163.M47   1992
909′.0974927—dc20   92-14666
                                                    CIP

English Translation © 1992 by Perseus Books Publishing, L.L.C.

Perseus Books is a member of the Perseus Books Group

Cover design by One Plus One Studio
Set in 11-point Bembo by Shephard Poorman Communications, Inc.

5 6 7 8 9   0201

Find us on the World Wide Web at
http://www.perseusbooksgroup.com

Contents

Islam and Democracy

Introduction
The Gulf War: Fear and Its Boundaries

The Gulf War is over. The soldiers have long since returned to
their bases. But for many people, and I am among them, this war is
one of those things that have no end, like symbolic wounds and
incurable illnesses. To be sure, life goes on. You are surprised to
find yourself singing in the springtime, putting a flower in your
hair, trying a new lipstick. Life continues, apparently as if nothing
had happened—except that occasionally, in an unfamiliar country
in the course of a morning reverie in a strange bed, something
cracks, and feelings and ideas coming from elsewhere burst into
consciousness. Then you realize that you have been tattooed somewhere with a nameless fear. A cut has been made, barely a scratch,
but all the more indelible because it is buried in the dark zones of
childhood terrors.

The first time this sort of thing happens you don't talk about it,
even to your closest friends. You try to forget it. You quietly sip
your coffee with the cultivated sensibility of those whose lot in life
is precarious, who develop a sort of apprehension about dreams,
especially dreams that fade too quickly. You touch the strange bed
to make sure it's real; you go to the window and try to make the
foreign city yours by studying the streets. Little by little, however,
you notice that you travel less and less in order to avoid things
foreign, and remembering your dreams becomes more and more
difficult. You accept this state of things in the hope of finding

peace and quiet, until the next incident, when even your own bed is transformed into foreign territory.

The most desperate outcry against the war was from women throughout the world, and especially from Arab women. A perhaps unnoticed detail, which nevertheless constitutes a historical breakthrough, is that during this conflict women, veiled or not, took the initiative in calling for peace—without waiting, as tradition demanded, for authorization from the political leaders, inevitably male. In Tunis, Rabat, and Algiers, women shouted out their fear louder than all the others; they were often the first to improvise sit-ins and marches, while the men could decide to do something only after drawn-out negotiations between various powers and minipowers. I participated in Rabat in dozens of meetings that spontaneously brought together intellectuals of all stripes to take a position against the war. When it was suggested that we go as a group to deliver a three- or four-paragraph communiqué to a foreign embassy or address a statement to a head of state, I was often astonished to see unfurled an unbelievable sequence of legal, diplomatic, and strategic ramifications of what seemed to me to be a rather simple gesture. Such ramifications would never have come to my mind, for as a woman the fact of being excluded from power gives me a wonderful freedom of thought—accompanied, alas, by an unbearable powerlessness.

Why did Arab women, usually silent and obedient, cry out their fear so strongly in that interminable night that was the war? Did they, whom the law officially designates as inferior, instinctively understand that that violence—presented as legitimate, and with the blessing of the highest authority defending human rights, the United Nations—would unleash within the Arab world other kinds of violence and legitimate the killing of others?

Did they shout because they felt, like sheep on the ʿid al-kabir (feast of the sacrifice), that that violence, directed by the priests of democracy and human rights, the Western heads of state and the high officials of the United Nations, augured an era of other rituals, rituals that would be more archaic and devastating than ever, that would hark back to other traditions, other ceremonies?

The lot of a woman in an Arab society that is at peace is precarious enough. But that lot is shaky indeed in an Arab society put to fire and sword by foreign forces.

How completely horrifying, then, are the prospects for a woman in an Arab society put to fire and sword in the name of international law and with the authorization of the Security Council of the United Nations! And what can be said when this is done by the very Western states that claim moral leadership of the world by forcing other nations to accept as universal the democratic model, which strips violence of all claim to legitimacy? Was this war inevitable? That is the question.

Why is the promise of democracy so threatening to hierarchies, why is it so destabilizing to Asian and African regimes, and why does it rally the holders of power around the appeal to the old traditions? Is it because the idea of democracy touches the very heart of what constitutes tradition in these societies: the possibility of draping violence in the cloak of the sacred? The West began to be considered credible for leadership of the nations it had traumatized through its own colonial terror when it promised to condemn all violence against humanity as illegitimate. The democratic model constituted a break with the sorry world of internal and interstate massacres and pogroms because it stood against violence and its legitimation.

Never had the Westerners, marked in the memory of the Third World by their past as brutal colonizers, succeeded in making themselves more credible as the bearers of good for other cultures than at the moment of the fall of the Berlin Wall. With the aid of the media, that event and the chain of falling despotisms which followed, especially the tragic and Ubuesque rout of Ceauçescu and above all the stillborn putsch in Moscow, stirred up a wind of long repressed hope in the Arab medinas. I remember the day when a fishmonger in the Rabat medina left me standing with my kilo of marlin in hand while he rushed to the neighboring shop, which had a television set, to hear the announcer report the capture of Nicolae and Elena Ceauçescu. When he returned after ten minutes and I expressed my displeasure to him at being abandoned, he gave me a reply that suggests what this moment meant to the masses: "I had the choice between serving you, which would have brought me forty dirhams [five dollars], and watching the apocalypse. Don't you see that there is no comparison? Forty dirhams or the apocalypse? Who would choose forty dirhams? I am illiterate, Madame, but I can sense, just like you who are probably covered with diplomas, that history has come to a turning point."

The fall of the Berlin Wall and the collapse of the men, institutions, and symbols of the Eastern European despotisms were seen as having universal meaning, despite the fact that they were geographically and ethnically localized. It is true that only the Europeans, more exactly the Germans, were involved as actors. It was they whom we saw climb the wall, rejoice over the falling of that wall, break it into pieces, and wear those pieces as jewels, relics of demolished frontiers and of a ripped *hijab* (curtain, veil). If a child should play around at translating the expression "Iron Curtain" into Arabic, he would stumble on the word *hijab* and translate it as *al-hijab al-hadidi*. And he would be right, because the translation of the word "curtain" in the sense of something that divides space to impede traffic, is precisely *hijab*.[1] The shopkeepers in the North African medinas and the peasants in the Atlas Mountains had no trouble identifying with those young blonds of both sexes who were hugging, singing, and destroying the wall, drunk with freedom and the desire to put an end to authoritarianism. At the fall of the Berlin *hijab* a new word burst out in the medinas, a word as explosive as all the atomic bombs combined: *shaffafiyya* (transparency).

Excluded from power and leading a life as mutilated as the arbitrary politics that crushes them is inefficient, Arab youths of both sexes were suddenly interested in those people of the North who shouted in the streets for liberty and justice. The only idea they had of Germany was of a rich country where the strength of the deutsche mark caused the people to seek pleasure rather than brood over the fate of the poor. And suddenly here they saw them, animated by a feeling so familiar, so visceral, so fundamental, the yearning for justice and freedom that they thought to be solely the preoccupation of the excluded: "Allah! The Germans feel just like us. They love their poorer brothers and are freeing them," 'Ali, a merchant in the Suq al-Sabat, the shoe market in the Rabat medina, kept exclaiming.[2] He bought a black-and-white television set

4

for his shop three days after the fall of the wall: "Just in order to see the world, *Ustada* [professor], just to see." The West that we believed to be anesthetized by its luxury and libertinism opened up to emotions forgotten since the humanizing wave of 1968. An unforeseen Europe flashed onto Arab television screens: "*Kafir* [infidel] and humanist. Allah is great," murmured ʿAli, one eye on his shoes, the other on the screen.

In the days following the crumbling of Berlin's *hijab,* just before the bombing of Baghdad, Europeans emerged for the Arab masses as promoters of the democratic credo, which would solve the problem of violence and reduce its use. And then the powerful wave of universal hope raised by the Europeans' song to freedom and the promise to condemn violence was rudely and brutally dashed by this war. It was a war in which the nonplussed Arab masses witnessed in a few months, like some bad twist in a tale in the *Arabian Nights,* the putting to sleep of those humanistic European youths who had been singing of nonviolence. What they saw on their television screens was the appearance of another breed they had forgotten about: old generals with kepis and medals just like those of the colonial army, generals who enumerated with pride the tons of bombs they had dropped on Baghdad. Two weeks after the beginning of the bombing, ʿAli sold his black-and-white television set and gave the money to the Moroccan Red Crescent to buy medical supplies for Iraq: "I don't understand anything, *Ustada.* This is a matter between the big shots. They just have to settle it between themselves. The shoe merchants of Baghdad are not in it. Why bomb the people? Can you imagine what would happen if they dropped a bomb on the Suq al-Sabat? A mere firecracker would send the whole medina up in flames! I am forty-six years old. The last time I saw a kepi on a French general I was ten years old. It was in 1955, on the eve of independence. But the Americans with their machines—it's like in the movies! Except that—God help us—it is our brothers who are the target. I have nightmares. My wife forbids me to look at the TV."

Violation is obscene. But violation, just after having flaunted before the eyes of the victim the hope of a new era in which violence would have no place, is more cruel than anything the human mind can describe. It is this ambivalence of the Europeans

5

toward violence which has created confusion in people's minds (I am speaking in ethnic terms, for the Gulf War has thrown discussion back to the most archaic level, that of two tribes who camp on the two shores of the Mediterranean). I have never felt my colleagues in the North so frozen in their Europeanness and I so frozen in my Arabism, each so archaic in our irreducible difference, as during my trip to Germany and France during the war to participate in discussions that were supposed to establish a dialogue, but that in fact established nothing but our pitiful inability to breach the boundary between us, to see the other in all his or her difference without letting that difference threaten and frighten. For as long as difference is frightening, boundaries will be the law.

I was born in a harem, and I instinctively understood very young that behind every boundary something terrifying is hiding. It is fear, or rather fears, that I want to speak about in this book. About all sorts of fears that burst forth from everywhere, from within and from without, from the East and from the West, and that multiply ad infinitum with strange mirroring effects. About individual fears, but most of all about collective fears. The former lead to suicide, which in the end is a personal matter, but the latter lead directly to *fitna*, outbreaks of violence all the more murderous because they take place within the intimacy of the group.

In my group the boundaries are fixed in law. On this side of the Mediterranean they become *hudud*. The *hudud*, the sure and certain boundaries that enclose and protect when one feels fear, like those our ancestors built around the medinas, were shown by the Gulf War to be pointless, at least when under Arab control. How can an Arab woman, I ask, insist on raising with her own group her problem, which is the *hijab*? How can she demand the negotiation of new boundaries for the sexes if her group feels naked and vulnerable in a world where bombs in a fury of passion can single out Baghdad?

In the beginning, at the time of its founding in the second century of the Hejira (the eighth century A.D.), Baghdad was called *madinat al-salam*, City of Peace, recalling on earth the memory of Paradise, the *dar al-salam* (Abode of Peace) of the Koran (sura 6, v. 128; sura 10, v. 26). This was the name given to it by its founder, al-Mansur, the second Abbasid caliph (136–58/754–75),[3] the name he inscribed on his coins, weights, and the letters he wrote. To make the city safe and invulnerable to attack, his architects designed a circular plan. Did they know that before them the Sabaeans in southern Arabia built the temple to *siyasa* (politics) in the shape of a circle? The idea of boundaries, of *hudud,* was present in al-Mansur's paradise, not only because his main preoccupation was defense, but also because his ideal of a well-organized Muslim community was based on the recognition of boundaries to separate and control differences. To guarantee maximum security, in 157/773 he ordered that the market be transferred outside the circle so that the ungrateful, seditious populace would stay far from the palace. That was his idea of paradise on earth.

Have things changed since then? Twelve centuries later is not our little paradise, which we create every day, in the image of the *madinat al-salam?* Who among us is able to imagine a city of peace without boundaries, without separations, without *hudud,* without walls, without *hijabs*? Who among us walks in security, without boundaries? Yet, the war proved that all Arab cities, including present-day Baghdad, can offer us many different fantasies, but not boundaries. Our cities have been stripped of boundaries. And how is one to exist without *hudud?* Where is one to find a sense of security on a planet where even the "defense of freedom," as Mr. Bush calls it, can mobilize high-tech violence as lethal as it is mobile? Is it by chance that a house without security is called *'awra,* "naked," like a woman without a *hijab* (sura 33, v. 13)?[4]

Women who walk in the streets without the *hijab,* unveiled, are seen as out of bounds, beyond the norm. They are considered defenseless because they have left the boundaries of the harem, the forbidden and protected space, but also because they have ventured into areas that are not theirs. Another word used in the sermons of the imams to explain the dangers that mixing of the sexes presents to the Muslim city is *tabarruj,* borrowed, taken, like *'awra,* from military vocabulary. It comes from the word *burj,* "stronghold," "so called because it is high and very visible," says the dictionary. The charm of a woman who knows herself to be beautiful, makes herself beautiful, adorns herself, and goes out walking in the street without a *hijab* while rolling her hips is offensive (*tabarruj*).[5] Walking about freely with face uncovered is exhibiting oneself to

7

the eyes of the other, and men are defenseless against such temptation.

Muhsan, "protected ones," is the Arabic word for married people, who are protected from just this temptation since they guarantee each other sexual satisfaction. *Muhsan* is a legal concept; it comes into play in cases of adultery, where it can increase the penalty.[6] Married women and men are protected from the temptation of adultery. A *muhsana* is protected by the caresses and pleasure given her by her husband just as a city is protected by a *hisn* (citadel, fortress). She is protected not only physically, from the violence of other men who desire her, but above all from the temptations that might push her to transgress the *hudud,* Allah's limits. The sexual *hudud* draw the line against unbridled desire just as ramparts defend the medina.

However, these *hudud* have another function that is just as strategic and that explains the outcry of the imams against mixing of the sexes. They protect the city against individualism, the source of all trouble. The *hudud* inscribe in the flesh the basic order that makes it possible to walk peacefully in a city organized around the preeminence of the group, where individualism and desire are carefully hidden behind the *hijab,* maintained behind boundaries. It is in this context that we must situate the fixation on the *hijab* if we are to understand why its disappearance causes so much anxiety. The *hijab* is a metaphor for the *hudud,* the boundaries that separate and create order and stand for all the others, especially those that delimit *dar al-islam,* the land of Islam, and protect it from the rest of the world.

Our fin-de-siècle era resembles the apocalypse. Boundaries and standards seem to be disappearing. Interior space is scarcely distinguishable from exterior. The generation of young people in their twenties, singles in no hurry, stroll around by the millions in the Arab capitals, especially the women, with all their charms exposed, fragile prey because they are without *hisn.* Transgression of the boundary is almost certain: "man was created weak," says the Koran in verse 28 of sura 4.[7] That weakness, comment the imams, is *shahwa,* "desire," which from the beginning was considered a major problem. How is this Muslim man, already disconcerted by so many unforeseen events, a visitor in the theater of the universe, which he looks at like a stranger, to be kept from "follow[ing] vain desires" (sura 4, v. 27)? Boundaries, *hudud, hisn, burj,* symbolic or stone-built casbahs—all are meant to discourage enemies. The Muslim man had to be alert, on the defensive, with one eye on the *hudud* that hemmed in the women, the other on the frontiers of the empire. What happens when the two boundaries give way, and both at the same time? The enemy is no longer just on earth; he occupies the heavens and the stars and rules over time. He seduces one's wife, veiled or not, entering through the skylight of television. Bombs are only an incidental accessory for the new masters. Cruise missiles are for great occasions and the inevitable sacrifices. In normal times they nourish us with "software": advertising messages, teenage songs, everyday technical information, courses for earning diplomas, languages and codes to master. Our servitude is fluid, our humiliation anesthetizing.

It is true that Mecca is still the center of the world, even though it needs the American air force to protect it. But what can such a force protect against, against what deviation and confusion? What about the women in the city? What prayers should be said, to avert what violence? Who is afraid, and of whom, in a city without boundaries? What will become of the women in a city where the defense of the *hudud* is in the hands of foreigners?

How, and through what precise management of fears, will the military map be superimposed on the map of desire, and how will the two be maintained and reflect each other in order to weaken the Arab man, who is already so closely controlled by the electronic agenda? And who will pay the price for all these indistinct boundaries? Traditionally women were the designated victims of the rituals for reestablishing equilibrium. As soon as the city showed signs of disorder, the caliph ordered women to stay at home. Will it be we, the women living in the Muslim city, who will pay the price, we who bear the boundary against desire tattooed on our bodies? Will we be sacrificed for community security in the coming rituals to be performed by all those who are afraid to raise the real problem—the problem of individualism and responsibility, both sexual and political?

In the new post–Gulf War city, which will be anything but the *madinat al-salam,* what will happen to the women who cause fear because they have already gone beyond the boundaries and refused to accept them? How can one imagine a Baghdad in which security is possible despite the disappearance of the circle?

PART I

A Mutilated Modernity

1

Fear of the Foreign West

Gharb, the Arabic word for the West, is also the place of darkness
and the incomprehensible, always frightening. *Gharb* is the territory of the strange, the foreign (*gharib*). Everything that we don't
understand is frightening. "Foreignness" in Arabic has a very
strong spatial connotation, for *gharb* is the place where the sun sets
and where darkness awaits. It is in the West that the night snaps up
the sun and swallows it; then all terrors are possible. It is there that
gharaba (strangeness) has taken up its abode.[1]

When my aunt Halima introduced into her Friday night stories
a person called Gharib, the Stranger, my cousin 'Aziz tugged on
my braids, I tugged on Mina's; it suddenly became difficult to
breathe; we stopped chewing the roasted chickpeas. Instinctively
we knew that terrible things were going to happen in our elderly
aunt's peaceful living room. In the *gharb* everything is engulfed in
darkness. One cannot see; one has to rely on the other senses to
make out what is moving, what might be dangerous. The place of
the setting sun is always a distant place, different from where we
live. It is also the territory of night. In Arabic the crow is called
ghurab, and it brings misfortune because its color heralds blindness.

The territory of the setting sun is also the territory of the far-
away, of what is elsewhere. The Maghrib is the country of the
setting sun. In the *Arabian Nights* the Maghribians were users of
magic, of everything that Islam forbids and bans. The accepted
name for Morocco is *al-maghrib al-aqsa,* the Far West. Within the
Arab community, we Maghribians are perceived by the people of

13

al-mashriq (the rising sun) as essentially shady; living close to the border of Christianity, we belong to the frontier territory. Is it because of our Berber heritage, because before the Arab conquest we spoke a different language and had different cults and rites? Is it because Tangier is only a few miles from Spain? Is it because before the discovery of America the Atlantic was considered the end of the world? But the difference does exist, and it will play a role as the Arab world is challenged to democratize itself and experience its many parts as riches to explore. When a Frenchman says "les Maghrébins," he is simply saying "foreigners."

Above all else, the strange, the foreign is spatial in concept. To protect against what is not understood, it is necessary to erect boundaries. The Gulf War taught the Arabs these two lessons at least: first, no border can any longer protect us from the *gharb;* and second, since we have a certain degree of vulnerability to start with, the terror that besets us becomes unbearable; facing what frightens us and understanding it is the only possible reflex. We are tired of being afraid. The medina and its inhabitants have finally decided to change the basic rules of the game: we must understand in order not to go under. It is not up to the foreign West to understand us; it is up to us to understand the West. We are well equipped for the job: millions of Arabs speak the languages of the West and are intimately familiar with its ideas, cultures, and dreams; millions of others live in its various countries and can mirror them back to us.

CONFRONTING FEAR

Until now the Arabs have been preoccupied with boundaries, with their uniqueness—what made them distinctive. Now they are simply trying to see what the other is. Why is the West so strong, and why are we so weak and vulnerable? Certainly democracy and respect for the individual and his rights have been recognized as the secret of the West's strength. A demand for these ideals emerged in the slogans of the masses who marched in the streets of Algiers, Tunis, and Rabat to protest the war and the bombing of

Baghdad. The Moroccans marching for peace on February 3, 1991, chanted:

Ma sa'alunash! Ma sa'alunash!
Al-qarar qararna!
Ma sa'alunash! Ma sa'alunash!

They didn't consult us! They didn't consult us!
The decision belongs to us!
They didn't consult us! They didn't consult us!

When the masses shout their desire for democracy, fear enters the corridors of entrenched power. Those who have control over *qarar* (decision making) will naturally try to transfer the ancestral fear of the West onto the idea of democracy itself, that strange, fascinating daughter the West had a part in bringing into the world. Identifying democracy as a Western malady, decking it out in the chador of foreignness, is a strategic operation worth millions of petrodollars. This little book will have attained its objective if it succeeds in suggesting some of the techniques used in this operation, including manipulation of fears by pasting ancient anxieties onto modern ones. It is a complex undertaking because it builds on unpredictable emotional elements like hope, desire and the promise of pleasure, and fear of pain. Mosque and satellite, sin and Coca-Cola, spiritual retreat and bank accounts: here we have the most Oriental sophistication, where one can hope for anything except simple answers. You can choose any colors you want, except black and white.

But let us proceed without haste, with lots of patience, and taking time for all the detours, because maybe they will lead beyond where the main roads end. I don't guarantee that the reader will be able to understand everything about the conflict between Islam and democracy; only the imams and presidents of the Muslim republics can give that kind of certainty. But by exploring the ambiguities, the analogies, and the paradoxes, as a woman I know that the ancestral locks and the fears that they are guarding can be unbolted.

15

Since the West spins fear the way a spider spins its web, it is enough to lure an idea into that web for it to take on the smell of fear and have the sound of forbidden things. Imagine for a moment a river on which two boats, the Orient and the Occident, are sailing toward each other, both with many people on board. The Orient looks at what is ahead of it, and suddenly it sees only its own reflection. The Occident at that precise moment is nothing but a mirror. The Orient is seized by terror, not because the Occident is different, but because it reflects and exhibits the very part of the Orient that it is trying to hide from itself: individual responsibility. Democracy—that is, insistence on the sovereignty of the individual rather than of an arbitrary leader—is not as new as the imams proclaim. What it is is repressed. Democracy in this sense is not foreign to the Muslim East; it is an infected wound that the East has been carrying for centuries. Opposition forces have constantly rebelled and tried to kill the leader, and he has always tried to obliterate them. This dance of death between authority and individuality is for the Muslim repressed, for it is soaked in the blood and violence that no civilization lets float to the surface; it is awash in the inexhaustible rivers of blood that our teachers hid from us and that we hid from ourselves while rhapsodizing about the benefits of unity and solidarity within the *umma,* the Muslim community. The West is frightening because it obliges the Muslims to exhume the bodies of all the opponents, both religious and profane, intellectuals and obscure artisans, who were massacred by the caliphs, all those who were condemned, like the Sufis and the philosophers, because, the palace said, they talked about foreign ideas from Greece, India, and ancient Persia.

The pouring of the masses onto the streets during the Gulf War, their calling for democracy, passed unnoticed in the Western media. Nevertheless, it was one of the essential events that will determine the future dynamics of the region. But the West and its cameras, focused behind another *hijab* and on other fears, sees in the Arab world only the dawn of obscurantist fanaticism. I was in the crowd that TV5, a European network, covered on February 3 in Rabat during the march for solidarity with Iraq. The French commentator presented it as a demonstration by xenophobic fundamentalists in which the French flag was burned. It is true that the French flag was burned and fundamentalists were among the demonstrators, but many other groups were present, including all the branches of the Moroccan Left and thousands of independents like me, of all persuasions, from university students and professors to shopkeepers. 'Ali, the shoe merchant from the Suq al-Sabat, was there. He is as independent as I am: "I don't have confidence in anyone, bearded or shaved," he often says.

THE CALIPH COMES FACE TO FACE WITH HIMSELF

Let us return to the river and the reflection and especially to that place of strangeness par excellence: ourselves. In one of the tales of the *Arabian Nights* the sovereign has the uncanny experience of meeting himself. Seeing his double on a river is for him complete disorientation, the most incomprehensible (*'ajib*) thing that could happen. The sovereign was none other than Harun al-Rashid (170–93/786–809), the fifth caliph of the Abbasid dynasty, whose life of magnificence and ostentation fired the imagination of his contemporaries:

> It is related that the Caliph Harun al-Rashid, was one night restless with extreme restlessness, so he summoned his Wazir Ja'afar the Barmecide, and said to him, "My breast is straitened and I have a desire to divert myself to-night by walking about the streets of Baghdad. . . . " He answered, "Hearkening and obedience." They rose at once and doffing the rich raiment they wore, donned merchants' habits and sallied forth three in number, the Caliph, Ja'afar and Masrur the sworder. Then they walked from place to place, till they came to the Tigris and saw an old man sitting in a boat. . . .

The disguised caliph and his attendants ordered the old man to take them for a ride on the river, offering him a handsome payment. But the old man refused, saying,

"The Caliph Harun al-Rashid every night cometh down Tigris-stream in his state-barge and with him one crying aloud: 'Ho, ye people all, great and small, gentle and simple, men and boys, whoso is found in a boat on the Tigris by night, I will strike off his head or hang him to the mast of his craft!' "

Then the old man pointed out the barge coming down the river in midstream, and they saw

> in the bows of the barge, a man holding in hand a cresset of red gold. . . . And they sighted in the stern another man, clad like the first and bearing a like cresset, and in the barge were two hundred white slaves, standing ranged to the right and left; and in the middle a throne of red gold, whereupon sat a handsome young man, like the moon, clad in a dress of black [the royal color of the Abbasids], embroidered with yellow gold. Before him they beheld a man, as he were the Wazir Ja'afar, and at his head stood an eunuch, as he were Masrur, with a drawn sword in his hand. . . . Then [the Caliph] examined the young man who sat on the throne and . . . said to Ja'afar, "Verily, this young man abateth nor jot nor tittle of the state of the Caliphate!"[2]

And the Commander of the Faithful said to Ja'afar, "By Allah, O Ja'afar, my reason is confounded and I am filled with amazement at this matter"[3] Nothing is more disturbing than to "see oneself" without having previously repressed anything. How should we react when destiny brings us face to face with ourselves? One can go crazy over less than that. The most incomprehensible stranger is that *gharib* who lives within us, buried in the deepest levels of our private selves. Compared to that foreignness, the rest is easy to probe.

Democracy is like that sovereign boat that floats on the river of time, obliging us to face what we have been unable to contemplate up to now in our Muslim culture: *'aql* (reason) and *ra'y* (personal opinion or judgment).[4] Since the beginning Muslims have given their lives to pose and solve the question that has remained an enigma up until the present: to obey or to reason, to believe or to

18

think? The assertion that the individual and his freedom are not the sole property of the West is at the heart of our tradition, but it has been submerged in incessant bloodbaths. The West with its insistence on democracy seems to us eminently *gharib,* foreign, because it is a mirror of what frightens us, the wound that fifteen centuries have not succeeded in binding: the fact that personal opinion always brings violence. Under the terror of the sword, political despotism has obliged Muslims to defer discussion about responsibility, freedom to think, and the impossibility of blind obedience. That was called the closing of the gates of *ijtihad,* "private initiative."

The *gharb,* by constantly talking about democracy, brings before our eyes the phantom ship of those who were decapitated for refusing to obey. It also brings to the surface the struggle between the pen and the sword: that is, the struggle between, on the one hand, the intellectuals, the *qadis* (judges) thirsting for justice, the Sufis thirsting for freedom, and the poets who tried to express their individuality; and, on the other hand, the caliphs and their *shariʿa,* their very authoritarian reading of divine law.

The West compels Muslims to remember Imam Malik Ibn Anas, the founder of the Malikite school, which we adhere to in North Africa. He died in the year 179 of the Hejira as a result of torture ordered by the caliph: "The governor of Medina summoned him and tried to make him take back his words. When he refused, the governor ordered him stripped naked and whipped. His hand [which held the pen] was beaten so badly that his shoulder was dislocated." Imam Malik still refused to take back his words. That was in year 147. It isn't important to know what his words were: the essential thing is that they expressed his opinion, which was different from the caliph's. Imam Malik never recovered from his beating; he lived on as a cripple, continuing to write and to struggle, until he finally died as a result of his injuries.[5]

The West, which constantly talks about democracy via its satellites and media networks, is frightening to some because it awakens the memory of forgotten greats of the past who are never celebrated by today's leaders. They were the defenders of that little thing, so fragile, so vulnerable, called *karama,* "dignity." There was Hallaj, the Sufi who insisted that the human being is the

19

depository of *haqq,* "truth," and that each person reflects divine beauty and as a result is necessarily sovereign. Hallaj was burned alive in Baghdad in year 390 of the Hejira (the eleventh century A.D.) because he asked, for example, why the earth and its inhabitants were so estranged from the divine.

Since only closeness to or remoteness from the divine can legitimate the authority of the imam, he has no authority if everyone is as close to God as he is. Hallaj insisted on the privilege of the human being to be a creature of God and, as such, capable of self-guidance since he is endowed with reason and reflects the remarkable power and grandeur of the intellect. He thus challenged authority simply by declaring that he was *al-haqq,* truth incarnate. His *"ana al-haqq"* ("I am truth") did not fall on deaf ears. Hallaj and his ideas were discussed in the streets and bazaars of Baghdad. The street gawkers were present on the day of his torture, which was of course public so that everyone would understand the caliph's action. If human beings claim that they are worthy of their God and that they can very well understand the truth by themselves, then of what use are the caliph and the imam and all the violence they inflict? It was not easy for the caliph to decide to execute Hallaj, because what Hallaj said made sense to many people. "He received a thousand blows and didn't utter a word. . . . The executioner cut off his hands and feet, cut off his head, which he kept aside, and then burned the body. When it was nothing but ashes, he threw it into the Tigris and planted the head on Baghdad's bridge."[6] As he was being tortured Hallaj chanted, *"Ana al-haqq."*

Who wants to remember? Who wants to disinter the bodies of the past and look back into that distant gloomy dawn when the cry for individuality and dignity was stifled in blood? How are we to flee from the wound within ourselves that we thought scarred over and long forgotten? If we had a true understanding of our past, we would feel less alienated by the West and its democracy. Does the *gharb* frighten the ruling despots, and the mini-despots who dream of replacing them, because it obliges them to plunge into that extraordinary quest for the Arab's truncated individuality?

The Universal Declaration of Human Rights doesn't frighten people because it declares that "the will of the people shall be the basis of the authority of government" and that "everyone has the right to take part in the government of his country." It is frightening because it awakens the memory of the Kharijites, that rebel sect that emerged at the beginning of Islamic history which is linked in our memory to terrorism and anarchy.

Side by side with the Sufis, who philosophized about the need to reject the idea of blind submission, another movement arose whose members were devoted to assassinating the imams who displeased them. Throughout its history Islam has been marked by two trends: an intellectual trend that speculated on the philosophical foundations of the world and humanity, and another trend that turned political challenge violent by resort to force. The first tradition was that of the *falasifa,* the Hellenized philosophers, and of the Sufis, who drew from Persian and Indian culture; the second was the Kharijite tradition of political subversion.

The Kharijites (seceders) never dreamed of changing the relationship between the leader and the community; they simply thought that by rebelling against the imam and sometimes killing him they could change things. The *falasifa* and the Sufis proposed a profound reflection on the nature of humanity and the nature of the divine, thus bringing up the question of the place of reason and personal opinion, as did the Western philosophers of the Enlightenment. The two traditions raised the same issues that we are today told are imports from the West, issues that Islam has never resolved: that of *taʿa* (obedience to the imam, the leader of the community) and that of individual freedom. Political Islam resolved these issues neither in theory (for debate was always stifled by the caliph) nor in practice, for the idea of representation was never effected, although the idea that the imam is chosen by the community is deeply rooted in Sunni Islam.

The *gharib* is still *ʿajib.* The strange is always fascinating, and as in the tales of the *Arabian Nights,* one never knows what foot to stand on when faced with the unusual. Something that fascinates you, but that you don't understand, can eventually destroy you. Western democracy, although it seems to carry within it the seeds of life, is too linked in our history with the seeds of death. But the death of whom? Of the authoritarian technocrats or the powerless intellectuals? Of the officials who are the watchdogs or the people who raise the challenge?

21

2

Fear of the Imam

The imam, who leads the *umma* (community) along the right path—that almost mythical figure who has fascinated Western television audiences since the spectacular entry of the Ayatollah Khomeini onto the scene in the 1970s—is not a strong man in Muslim political theory. From the beginning of Islam he was meant to be a vulnerable, challengeable leader, which often earned him assassination. But the extreme vulnerability that was an important component of the imamate—the theory of the ideal leader and the relationship between leader and followers—has disappeared in modern Islam, which politicians shamelessly manipulate to hide their anachronistic personal desire to exercise a narrow authoritarianism.

Whether they are now established leaders or challengers who want to replace the established leaders and flaunt promises of spirituality, the politicians who have used Islam have succeeded by recognizing the impossibility of advocating straight-out authoritarianism. Who will vote for a leader who cries from the rooftops that he wants to suppress the individual's right to make decisions? By promising on the contrary that if he becomes leader he will act like an imam, the modern politician mobilizes fifteen centuries of hopes. The ideal imam is just because he is attentive to the needs of the community and actively involved in people's well-being. But according to the ideal, the imam is just only because he is vulnerable and challengeable. Today that vulnerability has disappeared from the scene through the combined effect of two phenomena:

22

the separation of Muslim memory from the rationalist tradition of Islam, and the modern media. These two phenomena have given birth to a monstrosity: the all-powerful, unchallenged, unchallengeable media imam.

THE MEDIA IMAM AND THE TRADITIONAL IMAM

We can distinguish between two types of imam: the type created by the modern media, one who uses the media to create himself, versus the imam in the tradition of the Prophet, that is, the ideal imam described in the Koran and whose characteristics were later systematized in the political theory of the imamate and the caliphate, the visionary leader of the Muslim community. There is, of course, a great difference between these two imams. The media imam is strong, whereas the traditional imam is vulnerable. The media imam is the man we see on the screen explaining that he draws his power from God. The traditional imam did the same thing, but before the existence of television. This is an important distinction, because television cannot show complexities; it selects a detail, which then becomes enormous and takes over the whole screen. This technological effect is disastrous for our ideal imam. His vulnerability has disappeared in some way or other, if only because an imam and his opponent are never systematically interviewed on television. However, an imam always has an opponent. Neglecting this fact means shuffling the cards, and where politics is concerned, shuffling the cards necessarily gives the advantage to the one in power. This is what makes it essential to restore to our modern-day Caesars what they lack: their vulnerability. It must be restored if we are to understand the emotions at play today, with intolerance being absolutely pivotal.

The words "imam" and "caliph" both mean leader of the Muslim community. The difference is that the first is based on a spatial conception and the second on a temporal one. The imam is the person who is "in front of"; he occupies the leading place. The caliph is the successor to the Prophet, the one who takes his place as governor of the faithful. Often the word "imam" is used to designate the one who leads the prayers, whereas the caliph has

23

other duties (executing justice, directing the army, etc.) in addition to leading the prayers. One may say that a caliph is always an imam (he leads the prayers), but an imam is not necessarily a caliph. He might simply be a small-time official who leads the prayers in the neighborhood mosque. In the beginning the two functions were linked; the caliph necessarily had to lead the prayers. But very quickly the functions were separated. The caliph assigned someone else to fulfill the duties of imam in his place. Nevertheless, when they refer to leadership in the political sense, "imam" and "caliph" are synonymous.[1]

Bernard Lewis rightly points out that the office of ayatollah is a nineteenth-century creation in Iran, and that the "reign of Khomeini" is a twentieth-century innovation.[2] An imam who comes to power through cassette tapes sent from exile in France is certainly not some musty survivor of medieval tradition. It is true that we don't know much about the Islamic Middle Ages—though we can go so far as to state that imams did not have cassette tapes. We can also guess that our ignorance is far from being an accident; its cultivation is in fact a key political card which reflects a precise plan. For how can we evaluate which "Muslim identity" among those the politicians are selling is the authentic one if we don't have a deep understanding of our history?

Not only are the fundamentalist states, which base their political legitimacy on the past, not committed to understanding Islamic history; they also censor the books that try to clarify it. In that part of the Muslim world which has fabulous resources as its disposal from oil sales, no plans exist for museums or archival collections or serious archeological excavations. What is most striking about "museums" in Islamic countries, whether in Lahore, Dakar, or Rabat, is the amount of dust on the meager number of works one finds, and the monastic silence surrounding the few custodians on duty. You almost feel a need to apologize for disturbing them, and the incredible number of bureaucratic steps required to make a photocopy or buy a reproduction makes you want to leave empty-handed and go home to fantasize quietly about the past.

Islam is probably the only monotheistic religion in which scholarly exploration is systematically discouraged, if not forbidden, since rational analysis would not serve the purposes of the despots.

The Muslim history we possess is that ordered by the viziers to fulfill the needs of the caliphal palaces. Passing over in silence what the people think of the imam is a priority in that writing of history. One of the things which that history has tried to bury is fear of the imam—not just the fear he inspired, but also the fear he always carried deep within his thoughts, like a tyrannical lover.

Perhaps the world has never seen a power as fragile as that of the imam. He is owed obedience (*ta'a*) only if he is just (*'adil*). In the Koran the imam is sometimes a man and sometimes, as in sura 15, verse 19, a "high road plain to see" (*imam mubin*). A just imam must follow the road already laid out which leads the community to happiness on earth and in the Beyond. The importance of such a preestablished way of acting is that it gives the imam credibility in the eyes of Muslims, which is why *shari'a* (divine law) also means "the road." A politician who gives himself the name of imam in order to deal harshly with the members of the community and strip them of their rights certainly does not conform to the ideal of the *'adil* imam, the just ruler. Few imams have managed to lead the community to happiness, and many have died because of it, killed by dissatisfied followers. In Islam the words that relate to power and the relationship between ruler and ruled are spatial. This point will come up often because it forms the crux of the anxiety that the idea of instituting modern Western-style democracy arouses. Democracy recognizes no prescribed path to be followed, because such prescriptiveness would curtail individual freedom.

As must those of women, the acts of the imam must be within the *hudud,* Allah's limits. If the imam violates the limits, say some sects, he is subject to being killed. This vulnerability is completely absent from the modern media image of the imam. Two needs are superimposed on that image. First there is the need of the Western journalist, who wants to inform his audience as quickly as possible and to give a simple, clear description of what is happening in our part of the world; and there is the need of the political leader who claims the title of imam, who wants to be filmed and interviewed, and who has a precise message to sell—the message of the *ta'a* that Muslims owe him. If these two needs are not kept carefully distinct, we will not understand anything about that "despotic and fanatic Islam," a media construct that is easily conveyed but that neglects many important historical and symbolic mechanisms. It is those mechanisms, which are so often neglected by the media, that I wish to introduce here to restore a more nuanced image of Islam, an image in which the small details count and help produce more precise contours.

Today Islam is presented as a bastion of fanatical despotism in which reason has no place. Passive Muslims thoughtlessly obey the imam. For at least two reasons, nothing is more false than this notion of the fanaticism of Muslims. First, the history of Islam's leaders is a sorry tale of one political assassination after another, the killing of the imam by malcontents among the faithful. I call that trend the "tradition of rebel Islam," a sort of spontaneous democracy, or "people power," that reacted by killing the leader without putting much thought into how to bring about basic changes. Alongside the rebel tradition of revolt focused on the person of the leader was another form of dissidence, the "rationalist tradition." This tradition proposed reintroducing reason (*'aql*) and personal opinion (*ra'y*) into the political process.

This rationalist tradition has had its defenders and martyrs, the best known being the Mu'tazila, who raised the question of *qadar* (predestination), that is, the question of whether individuals are responsible for their acts. This rationalist tradition considered *'aql* a precious endowment, and its defenders glow in our history against a seamy background of political intrigue. The Mu'tazila were systematically combated by the holders of power, who condemned them as *falasifa* (philosophers) who were "polluting" Islam with the humanistic patrimony of ancient Greece.

From the first centuries of Islam the Mu'tazila were castigated as being in the service of foreigners and the propagators of enemy ideas. As such they were repudiated as *mulhidun* (atheists) who were perverting the faith. This condemnation of the humanistic spirit, which began with the Mu'tazila on the pretext that they were importing foreign ideas, has persisted throughout the centuries and continues still today. The difference is that the Greek influence was extended elsewhere, and now it is the whole West that is condemned as the source of borrowing and cultural importation. But the principle remains the same: for fifteen centuries Moslem politicians have censored intellectuals who wanted to synthe-

26

size the humanistic traditions by labeling as polluting the very thing that creates the dynamic of all civilization: its capacity to assimilate and use new ideas and accomplishments of the human spirit. Nevertheless, the fact that the rationalist, humanistic tradition was rejected by despotic politicians does not mean that it doesn't exist. Having an arm amputated is not the same as being born with an arm missing. Studies of amputees show that the amputated member remains present in the person's mind. The more our rational faculty is suppressed, the more obsessed we are by it. But first let us examine the rebel tradition.

THE REBEL TRADITION: THE KHARIJITES

It is difficult to imagine a weaker political leader than a Muslim imam. The ideal imam is modest, trembling with fear before his God and terrified before those he governs, for making an unjust decision will lead him directly to hell. An outraged believer is capable of anything. In theory, it is the Muslim's duty to revolt against an imam who makes unjust decisions, and some sects quickly decreed that he should be assassinated. This rebel tradition is one of the most primitive that Islamic societies have known.

Beginning in the first decades after the death of the Prophet, the Kharijites raised the question of whether you must obey the imam if he does not protect your rights. Should you blindly obey, or can you trust your own judgment? The Kharijites answered by saying that you are not obliged to obey; you can "go out" (*kharaja*) from obedience. "To go out" is the title they gave themselves, one that has stuck to all dissident movements: "Any person who goes out [*kharaja*] from obedience to a just imam whom the community has chosen is called *khariji*," explains Shahrastani.[3] The motto of the Kharijites, "*La hikma illa lillah*" ("Power belongs only to God"), was used for the first time during the fourth caliphate, that of ʿAli, and led to his assassination by terrorists sent by the Kharijites in year 40 of the Hejira (661). This same slogan has condemned hundreds of imams and Muslim leaders, the last of whom was President Anwar Sadat of Egypt. Political dissidence is expressed in

Islam as condemnation of the leader. It is this rebel tradition that links dissidence with terrorism.

The Kharijites, who intimidated Muslim populations for centuries, initiated the use of terrorism as an answer to arbitrary rule. Because they did not agree with the imam, ʿAli, they decided to assassinate him. In 40/660 a band of Kharijites meeting in Mecca decided on the victims and the killers. The one who was to kill ʿAli, Ibn Muljam, was directed to go to Kufa, where he would find his victim. The mosque was to be the site of the execution, since the caliph went there at dawn every day to lead the prayers. One member of the team charged with the assassination was a woman, Qatami: "On the night of Friday 13 Ramadan [January 20, 661] that woman withdrew for prayer under a sort of mosquito net within the walls of the great mosque. . . . She brought a piece of silk which she cut into strips and put around the men's foreheads, while the men took their swords and went to sit facing the door through which ʿAli would enter the mosque, as he did every morning at the first call of the muezzin." When the muezzin's call to prayer rang out, everything happened as planned: "ʿAli came out of his house and called out in a loud voice, 'Muslims, come to prayer, come to prayer!' Ibn Muljam and his accomplices threw themselves on him. . . . Ibn Muljam struck him a sword blow on the top of his head." Thus was violence established as the corollary of dissidence. One detail in the account of al-Masʿudi summarizes the tragedy of political Islam: "It is reported that ʿAli had kept watch that whole night before the murder and that he kept repeating as he paced from the door to his bedroom, 'God knows that I have never lied, nor been accused of lying.' "[4] This heartrending cry, even if it comes from the imagination of al-Masʿudi (who was known for his exaggerations), perfectly summarizes the weakness of the imam, which today is hidden from view.

Many Kharijite sects advocated anarchy as a solution; getting rid of the leader came to be an acceptable tactic.[5] This was preached by the Najadat, the followers of Najda Ibn ʿAmir who were one of the most extreme sects: "The Najadat were in agreement that in fact the people did not really need an imam. They had only to organize themselves to ensure justice.[6] Najda Ibn ʿAmir was assassinated in year 69 of the Hejira, fifty-nine years after the death of the Prophet. Condemnation of a leader is pronounced in the name of *ʿadala* (justice) and to bring a stop to *munkar* (injustice). *ʿAdala* and *munkar* are key words in the slogans of contemporary Islamic dissidence, which is repudiated by Qadi ʿAshmawi, the Egyptian religious authority and author of the caustic *Al-Islam al-siyasi* (Political Islam), as stemming from the Kharijite tradition. ʿAshmawi rejects both words as an ossification (*tajmid*) of conflict which reduces it to a matter of the leader, and then ends up in excluding the masses from decision making.[7] According to ʿAshmawi, seeking justice through violent subversion removes the essential element from the scene: the masses and their will. The Prophet's ideal, according to his *risala* (the message of the revealed Koran), ʿAshmawi says, is to struggle against the despot (*taghiya*), but without violence. This necessarily puts responsibility on the masses. We will have occasion to come back to this point in Chapter 7, on individualism.

The murder of imams began very early, even before the caliphate of ʿAli. What began with ʿAli was political terrorism—killing as a plan and a program.

The first caliph to be assassinated was, paradoxically, the figure with the greatest reputation for justice, ʿUmar Ibn al-Khattab, the second orthodox caliph, who reflected deeply on his mission. He was one of the supporters of *raʾy*, individual judgment, as the source of decision making. That word was to become a fundamental concept in the rationalist tradition. ʿUmar is only the first on a very long list of assassinated imams. That compiled by Ibn Hazm in his chapter "Those Among the Caliphs Who Died by Assassination and the Manner in Which They Were Killed" is one of the most fascinating.[8] The beginning of the list sets the tone:

1. Caliph ʿUmar Ibn al-Khattab: stabbed in 23/644. He was the second caliph to govern after the death of the Prophet.
2. Caliph ʿUthman: hacked to death by swords. ʿUthman was the third orthodox caliph, who took power after ʿUmar and was assassinated in 35/656.[9]
3. Caliph Marwan Ibn al-Hakam: smothered by his wife, Umm Khalid. Fourth caliph of the Umayyad dynasty, he died in 64/683.

4. ʿUmar Ibn ʿAbd al-ʿAziz: "poisoned, they say."[10] ʿUmar was the eighth Umayyad caliph; he died in 101/720.
5. Al-Walid Ibn Yazid: hacked to death.

A number of the assassinated caliphs, according to Ibn Hazm's list, were slashed by many swords—that is, they were the victims of the anger of a group in a killing that had the air of ritual. There were some odd cases, like the death of al-Hadi, the brother of Harun al-Rashid, who during an outing had the idea of swinging one of his courtiers over a precipice. The courtier hung on to al-Hadi, and the two fell to their deaths together.[11] In most cases, however, the imam was a sort of sacrificial victim. A psychoanalytic study of regicide (or rather "imamicide"), which has yet to be done, would be filled with information about the morbid fascination that the leader inspires. In general, murder of the leader is the business of men, although women like Umm Khalid, the wife of Marwan Ibn al-Hakam, have committed assassinations from time to time. Rather than the sword, they use cushions or poison, or sometimes they choose the *hammam* (bath) as the site of the murder.[12]

Taking the place of the leader because the rebel believes he can do better is the fantasy and the motive that for fifteen centuries have inspired scores if not hundreds of sects. The modern militant opposition forces who claim power in the name of the sacred are only replaying that scenario. The traditional palace revolt is a matter between a ruler and a rebel chief and leaves the masses of believers on the sideline. An anecdote about a caliph and a Sufi recounted by al-Masʿudi illustrates the structural weakness of Muslim thrones.

AL-MAʾMUN AND THE SUFI:
WHO GAVE YOU THIS THRONE?

Al-Maʾmun, the seventh Abbasid caliph (198–218/813–33), was one of the most powerful sovereigns of his time, and the magnificence of his reign and his marriage to Buran inspired countless tales. Nevertheless, in the eyes of one of his faithful followers, this man whose armies made the world tremble was just a man like any other, in no way empowered by the community to govern. This audacious thought, which lies in the hearts of all Muslims, came to the mind of a certain Sufi who had dedicated his life to meditation and the spiritual quest. He longed to ask the caliph what he thought about his throne:

> One day when the caliph was holding an audience his chamberlain, ʿAli Ibn Salih, appeared and said to him: "Commander of the Faithful, a man dressed in white garments of coarse material which he wears tucked up is at the palace gate. He asks to be admitted to take part in the discussions." I understood, continued Yahaya [the narrator, one of the witnesses of the scene, who remembered it and told it to others], that it was a Sufi, and I wanted to signal the caliph not to admit him. But he gave the order to let him enter.
>
> In came a man whose robe was tucked up in his belt and who held his sandals in his hand. He stopped at the edge of the carpet and said: "Greetings! May the mercy and blessings of God be upon you!" Al-Maʾmun returned the greeting. The stranger asked permission to approach the caliph, who granted it and invited him to be seated.
>
> Once seated, he said to the caliph: "Do you permit me to address you?"
>
> "Speak of what you know," al-Maʾmun told him, "for that is pleasing to God."
>
> The man then asked: "Do you owe this throne upon which you sit to the full consent of the Muslims, or rather to the violence that you have exercised on them, using your force and your power?"[13]

Intelligent and conscientious, al-Maʾmun responded with a preciseness that showed the respect he gave to this man who had the courage to be sincere with a caliph, who held so much more power than he. He said that he owed his throne neither to the consent of the Muslims (ʿijtimaʿ) nor to violence (mughalaba), but simply to the fact that he had received it from a "sultan" (a holder of earthly power) who had the throne before him and had passed it to him by

agreement.[14] The problem for al-Maʾmun lay in the fact that nowhere does the Koran mention hereditary power. Islam categori-
cally condemns it, as we shall see when we explore the idea of the
taghiya, the pre-Islamic tyrant.

The description of this meeting between the caliph and his ques-
tioner is moving because it lays open for all to see the great beauty
of Islam and the tragic weakness of its political system. No throne
is stable. Any person at all, however lowly, can call to account the
most powerful man of the city.

Two ways lay open to the Muslims: the way of rebellion taken
by the Kharijites, which leads to violence and murder; and the way
of *ʿaql,* glorifying reason, which began with the Muʿtazila, the
philosophers who intellectualized the political scene. Instead of
preaching violence against an unjust imam like the Kharijites, the
Muʿtazila held that the thinking individual could serve as a barrier
against arbitrary rule. Muslims would use both these approaches at
different times, both were extremely important, recurring
throughout the centuries. In the modern Islamic world only the
violent, rebellious way is being taken by those who loudly proclaim their wish to rule. The rationalist tradition is apparently not
part of their Muslim heritage. That is why outlining it and thinking about it is so critical.

THE RATIONALIST TRADITION: THE MUʿTAZILA AND *RAʾY*

The Muʿtazila moved the problem to the philosophical level, asking, What is the purpose of our existence on earth, and to what use
should we put *ʿaql,* that marvelous gift from heaven? If God has
created us intelligent, it is to carry out a plan. The rationalist opposition replaced the murder of the imam with the triumph of reason
as the barrier against despotism. To achieve the ideal of the well-
governed community, all the faithful must be enlisted as bearers of
God's most precious gift, the ability of the individual to think and
analyze. By introducing reason into the political theater, the
Muʿtazila forced Islam to imagine new relationships between ruler
and ruled, giving all the faithful an active part to play alongside the

palace. Politics was no longer just a Kharijite duel between two actors, the imam and the rebel leader. A third element came on the scene: all believers who are capable of reasoning. The two conflicting trends within Islam, Kharijite rebels and Muʿtazila philosophers, appeared on the scene very early and continued, under various names, to be active throughout Muslim history. Although their approaches differed, they shared one basic idea: the imam must be modest and must in no way turn to despotism. It was only on the subject of methods of realizing this ideal of the imamate that they diverged.

Both in the political theory of the imamate (the functioning of the institution) and in official Muslim history, the imam is weak. In theory obedience is required only if the imam follows the *shariʿa,* which leads to happiness, harmony, and prosperity. In ancient Arabic *sharaʿa* means "going toward the source of water," that is, toward the element that assures life and renews energy.[15] But Islam is based on an absolute prohibition against confusing God with man, so the obedience owed to the imam must in no way be considered equal to that owed to God. The imam is never infallible in Sunni (orthodox) Islam. This is a fundamental difference between Sunni and Shiʿa. A Khomeini, an imam who claims to be infallible, a leader who cannot err, is not exportable to the lands of Sunni Islam. This does not mean that the regimes in power there and the fundamentalist opposition groups basing themselves on the sacred don't dream of it. Certainly they fantasize about the extraordinary power of Imam Khomeini, but they cannot root that fantasy in any historical schema inherited from their ancestors, as can the Shiʿites. From the beginning, the power of the Shiʿite imam was quasi-supernatural, whereas Sunni Islam has been astonishingly pragmatic and hyper-rational. How is it possible to believe that a human being can avoid making mistakes?

The rationalist tradition of the Muʿtazila triumphed and succeeded in burying a corrupt dynasty, the Umayyads, through the insistence on the preeminence of *ʿaql.* Unlikely as it seems, the Abbasids came to power riding the fiery steed of triumphant reason, which the Muʿtazila proposed to a fantastic medieval Islam. Alas, very quickly the Abbasids fell into despotism, the Muʿtazila became pariahs and *ʿaql* a shriveled exile, and the Muslim world rolled toward the precipice of mediocrity, where it now vegetates—in the mediocrity that is tacked on us as the essence of our "authenticity."

How was it that politicians who fought against reason succeeded, and continue to succeed, in gutting one of the most promising religions in human history of its substance? The way of dissidence was prevalent within Islam from the beginning. But as intellectual opposition was repressed and silenced, only political rebellion and terrorism had any success, as we see so well today. Only the violence of the subversive could interact with the violence of the caliph. This pattern, which is found throughout Muslim history, explains the modern reality, in which only religious challenge preaching violence as its political language is capable of playing a credible role.

The Mu'tazila intellectuals were not only philosophers, mathematicians, engineers, doctors, and astronomers; they were also Sufis, who found in religious texts everything they needed to bolster the idea of the thinking, responsible individual. It must be remembered that in the beginning scientific investigation was necessarily linked to the flowering of mystical reflection, in that the best homage one could render to God was the good use of one's mind. The tension in Christianity in the early modern period between the church and scientific investigators, so well represented by Galileo's fate, does not exist in Islam in normal times. Rather, political ambushes are artificially created in times of crisis, as in the threats against Rushdie or the condemnation of great thinkers like the Egyptian Taha Husayn in the period after World War II.

Abu Zahra has systematized the various divergences that occurred in Islam within three categories: the political category (he includes the Kharijites here); the legal category, which established four schools of law, the Maliki, Shafi'i, Hanbali, and Hanafi; and the intellectuals, who focused on the very nature of belief, that is, the great philosophical questions like human destiny and the universe and its mysteries. He puts the Mu'tazila in the last category.[16]

One of the questions the Mu'tazila debated, and which drew crowds, was the question of *qadar*, "predestination": are we free (*qadir*) to act and thus responsible for our fate, or is our destiny already fixed by God? One branch of the Mu'tazila, the Qadiriyya, made this its central concern. Its adherents, the Qadiri, were "believers in free destiny, who thought that the human being was free to decide his own acts and so was responsible for everything he did, for evil as well as good." If God has fixed the destiny of men, he is then responsible for the evil that exists on earth. Either man is free, or God is responsible for evil. But the latter proposition is impossible: "For if God created evil, he would be unjust."[17]

However philosophical they were, the Mu'tazila found they couldn't avoid politics. If one is a reasonable, responsible being, one can obey authority only under certain conditions, notably under conditions of popular representation. Any authority that does not come from the people does not bind their will:

> The Mu'tazila and other schools maintain that the title of imam is obtained by the [free] vote of the nation. God and his Prophet, they say, did not designate a particular imam, and the Muslims were not obliged to give their vote to any specially designated man; rather, the choice is entrusted to the nation [*umma*]. It alone has the right to choose from among its members its own representative, to whom it delegates executive power.[18]

The entry of the Mu'tazila onto the political scene transformed and intellectualized it by bringing in new concepts: for example, *i'tizal*, that is, taking a middle position, weighing the pros and cons. This issue was important because it brought up the question of tolerance. What should be done with a Muslim who commits a sin? Should one condemn him or take a middle position, a position of neutrality? The Mu'tazila chose the second option—neutrality, and thus, tolerance. One cannot condemn someone without mature reflection on his conduct. This *i'tizal* was the inevitable result of respect for reason. The obedience/revolt pattern of the Kharijites was replaced by another: obedience (*ta'a*)/reason (*'aql*). The Abbasids adopted the Mu'tazila philosophy as their official doctrine for at least a century, the century of openness.[19] Openness meant embracing all human knowledge, including the scientific treatises and Greek philosophy now translated into Arabic.

Translation of the Greek humanistic heritage into Arabic started out as a government project under the caliph al-Ma'mun and was carried on throughout the ninth century. Hunayn Ibn Ishaq (d. 873), a Christian, founded a school of translators which recruited its staff from among the most brilliant intellectuals of Baghdad and the whole empire. But they didn't just translate the Hellenic heritage, as the Western stereotype depicts. They also turned to Iran and India to collect, translate, and synthesize everything that the genius of other cultures had accumulated before undertaking to augment and expand it. This importation and translation of foreign learning was enriched by original scholarship, producing the flowering of Muslim thought, which came to be known as *falsafa* (philosophy). Its practitioners, whether logicians, mathematicians, or physicians, were called *falasifa,* an all-inclusive term that later made their wholesale condemnation easy when the Abbasids succumbed to despotism and the cult of *ta'a,* relying only on the *ahl al-hadith* (Hadith people), religious authorities who stuck to a strict interpretation of the *shari'a,* knowledge revealed in Arabic.[20] Only this strictly limited interpretation, intended to affirm obedience as the main point, was fostered by the palace.

The activity of the *falasifa* was called *kalam* (discussion), not only because it was based on the logical exposition of arguments, but also because these new ideas poured into the suqs and became a preoccupation of the masses. At the beginning of the ninth century the Mu'tazila, with the blessing of the Abbasid court, orchestrated this scientific and speculative flowering. All the great names of scientific and philosophical learning belong to this era: al-Khwarizmi (d. 850), the father of algebra, a mathematician and astronomer; al-Kindi (d. 873), often called the first *faylasuf* (philosopher); al-Razi (d. 925), the great physician who was known in the West as Rhazes; al-Battani (d. 929), the father of trigonometry; and the metaphysician al-Farabi (d. 950), the author of *Al-madina al-fadila* (The Virtuous City).

But very early the Abbasid dynasty, which took power carrying the torch of reason and mobilized the most brilliant minds among the Mu'tazila to promote its propaganda, fell into palace intrigues. The result was that the opening to reason, personal opinion, and the cult of private initiative was condemned as a "foreign" enterprise. The *falasifa* were hunted down and the freethinkers condemned as infidels and atheists. To strengthen their despotic rule the Abbasids recruited their thinkers from the tradition of knowledge based on *ta'a,* banning reflection. This tradition is called the *shari'a,* creating the confusion that today blocks the democratic process by linking our blind obedience to the leader with our respect for religion. All calls for a rational relationship between the imam and his followers as well as any criticism of the leader are discredited as a rejection of Islam and a lack of respect for its principles and ideals. Thus in order to serve the needs of the Abbasid palace, the *shari'a* was stripped of its questioning, speculative dimension. The imam became a violent, bloodthirsty despot, and only the Kharijite rebel tradition managed to continue to assert itself as a voice of opposition.

After condemning the Mu'tazila as bearers of a foreign patrimony, the Abbasids of the period of despotism were assassinated by rebels from a Muslim *umma* cruelly deprived of *ra'y,* the right to one's own opinion. Greeks and Mu'tazila became vermin that had to be wiped out. The Muslim world rumbled on toward obscurantism, with its enlightened intellectuals being systematically condemned and its people reduced to intellectual apathy. From then on, fanatical revolt was the only form of challenge which survived within a truncated Islam.

It is that Islam of the palaces, bereft of its rationalist dimension, that has been forced on our consciousness as the Muslim heritage today. It is that Islam of princes and hangmen that was reactivated after independence from colonialism in the 1940s through 1960s. Beginning in the 1970s, petrodollars financed the propaganda that encouraged submission and repudiated reflection. One of the immediate results of that financing was the sight of militant fundamentalists in the very heart of Saudi Arabia with the spectacular takeover of the Great Mosque of Mecca in November 1979 by the followers of Juhayman Ibn Muhammad al-'Utaybi and Muhammad Ibn 'Abdallah al-Qahtani.[21] At the same time, the availability of oil money intensified the connection between official Islam, supported by the ideology of *ta'a,* and militant Islam. The latter, the heir of the rebel fringe, the Kharijite reaction, is the inevitable offspring of official despotism disguising itself as obedience to the divine will.

In the face of this convergence, Arab intellectuals, mostly philosophers, are defending the opening to all humanistic thought, whether ancient or modern. The rationalist past and the luminaries of Western humanism have been reclaimed, Marx among them. Contemporary philosophers and ideologues like Muhammad ʿAmara, Husayn Mruwa (who was killed a few years ago in Beirut), and Muhammad al-Jabiri (one of today's most important thinkers) have become more well known in the Arab world than hit singers and often more popular than the heads of state who try to repress them. The Moroccan al-Jabiri is probably the philosopher most read by Arab youths, if I can judge by the remarks of students in conference debates and informal discussions. In *Nahnu wa al-tharwa* (We and Our Heritage) he contends that the Muslims did not just pass the Greek heritage on to the West, but rather enlarged and enriched it.[22] His masterly *Taqwin al-ʿaql al-ʿarabi* (The Process of the Formation of Arab Thought), which takes up the question of the opposition between the obedience of the palace and the reason of the intellectuals, has reconciled millions of Arab young people to modernity and raised their democratic aspirations.[23] Devouring his books, they find there an Islam in which openness and personal opinion are an integral part of our tradition. This aspect of openness in our culture is ignored by the West. The works of al-Jabiri and the others are not translated, and their authors are not interviewed by Western television networks. Is it because al-Jabiri resembles a French or German intellectual, focusing on the great eternal values like integrity and self-respect, that he doesn't convey the facile exoticism the media look for to depict the frightening Islam that furthers racism and encourages rejection? It is certainly interesting to note that the leaders of fanatical movements are often invited to speak on television programs, while the whole progressive movement is ignored by the Western media, duplicating at the international level the media tactics of the local despots.

The Arab governments denounced reason (ʿaql) as foreign after the departure of the colonial powers. In the last few decades, the combination that all despots dream of—making obedience to the imam correspond to obedience to God—became the program and the law of the Arab regimes that base themselves on the sacred. The Muslim world of the 1980s, governed by leaders who attack reason, sank into *al-inhitat* (decay). Our military, economic, political, and ethical decline was brought to consciousness for us by the Gulf War, which CNN displayed before the eyes of the world, revealing Muslims as partially educated but deprived of *ra'y*.

In his amazing book *Al-milal wa al-nihal* (Revealed Religions and Fabricated Beliefs), written in the twelfth century, the Iranian Shahrastani crystallized the process by which reason was set aside. *Ta'a* (obedience to God) was to become forever confused with *milal* (revealed religions); everything else was only forgery, fabricated belief. It would thus affirm the triumph of the *ahl al-hadith,* the supporters of a rigid interpretation of the *shari'a,* which reduces Islamic civilization to revealed knowledge in the Arabic language only. The concept of reason and all speculation about personal opinion would ever after be dismissed as *nihal,* beliefs fabricated by sects. The word *nahala* means "to imitate," "to counterfeit"—in a word, "to forge." *Ra'y* was then forever connected to criminal activities that destroyed the solidarity of the *umma.* It is that Islam, shorn of its rational pole, that we are now being compelled to recognize as *thurat islami* (Muslim heritage), in the same terms used by Shahrastani: believe (*i'tiqad*) and obey (*ta'a*), or stick to one's own opinion and thus act in an egotistical way. This question has always been posed, and the way of responding to it has not changed since the twelfth century. It is the one that is being loudly proclaimed by those who propose despotism as a way of life: individuals' use of reason means weakening Islam and serving the enemy.

Shahrastani simplified things by saying that the world is divided in two: those who believe in one of the revealed religions, and those who rely on their individual inclination: "Those who believe something or say something only have two choices: either to adopt a belief, that is, to adhere to a preexisting idea and borrow it, or to fabricate one from one's own arrogant personal opinion." Since the time of 'Umar Ibn al-Khattab, all Muslim men and women conscious of their dignity have had to face the dilemma of whether to believe or to cultivate their own judgment. Shahrastani's solution was simple: "A Muslim is he who believes and obeys. Religion is obedience. An obeying Muslim is religious. He who gives priority to his own opinion is a modernizing innovator and a creator.[24]

Al-milal wa al-nihal contains all the terms of the debate on democracy which is shaking the Muslim world today and permeates the press of both the Left and the Right. The debate turns on six key words that constitute its two poles. On one end is the pole of allegiance to the leader, confounded with faithfulness to God; it inseparably links together three words: *din* (religion), *i'tiqad* (belief), and *ta'a* (obedience). At the other end are grouped together three words that are just as strategic and that all affirm individual responsibility: *ra'y* (personal opinion), *ihdath* (innovation, modernization), and *ibda'* (creation). The conflict lies in the fact that this second pole has for centuries been condemned as negative, subversive. Asserting oneself and believing in one's personal opinion mean weakening the palace and the power of the community concentrated in the hands of the caliph, and thus playing the enemy's game. This fear that the expression of individual opinion will weaken the group and play into the hands of adversaries is the emotional vein that all those who wish to block the democratic process in the Arab world try to exploit.

From the time of Shahrastani on, the definition of a Muslim, forged by political men faithful to the despotic regimes, relayed by the *fuqaha* (religious authorities), and serving the palaces, would condemn *ra'y, ihdath,* and *ibda'* as foreign and blasphemous. But this stripping our heritage of the rationalist tradition would not have succeeded if we had had access to the modern humanistic heritage that the Europeans forged during their bloody struggles against despotism, which opened the way to scientific development and political participation. With complete impunity, the Muslim leaders would battle the Muslim intellectuals who tried to explain and spread the philosophy of the Enlightenment. Like the Mu'tazila of the past, those intellectuals were harassed, condemned, and denounced as blasphemers during the nineteenth and twentieth centuries. Bans on their writings and imprisonment followed, despite the declarations of independence—but with one difference. The Mu'tazila were the traitors who imported Greek ideas; the modern intellectuals are called servants of the West. Twentieth-century humanism, celebrated elsewhere as the triumph of creativity and the flowering of the individual, is forbidden to us on the pretext that it is foreign. Obscurantism is proposed as the ideal of the future, and one to defend.

3

Fear of Democracy

Arabs do not so much have a fear of democracy as suffer from a lack of access to the most important advances of recent centuries, especially tolerance as principle and practice. By this I mean the secular humanism that has allowed the flowering of civil society in the West. Humanistic ideas—freedom of thought, the sovereignty of the individual, the right to freedom of action, tolerance—were propagated in the West through secular schools. With a few rare exceptions (notably Turkey), the modern Muslim state has never called itself secular, and has never committed itself to teaching individual initiative. On the contrary, individualism always held a rather ambiguous place among the "reformers" of the nineteenth-century nationalist movement. This movement, focused on the struggle against colonization and therefore viscerally anti-Western, was obliged to root itself more deeply than ever in Islam. Facing the militaristic, imperialistic West, Muslim nationalists were forced to take shelter in their past and erect it as a rampart—cultural *hudud* to exorcise colonial violence. The Muslim past they reactivated did not anchor modern identity in the rationalist tradition. In fact, the nationalists were prisoners of a historical situation that inevitably made modernity a no-win choice. Either they might construct modernity by claiming the humanistic heritage of the Western colonizer at the risk of losing unity (for when we speak about the rationalist tradition, we are talking about *ra'y,* "individual opinion," and *'aql,* "reason," and therefore about the possibility of divergence of opinion); or they could carefully safeguard a sense

42

of unity in the face of the colonizer by clinging to the past, favoring the tradition of *ta'a,* "obedience," and foreclosing all Western innovation.

Alas, it was this second solution that the nationalist politicians more or less involuntarily chose. The essence of the two rationalist heritages, both the Muslim and the Western, was freedom of thought, freedom to differ. This was sacrificed to save unity. What the politicians and reformers of the 1920s and 1930s didn't clearly see was that by shutting out reason, Muslims weakened themselves more than ever and became that crippled, powerless mass that the Gulf War spread before the world on television.

Once colonization had ended after World War II, the newly independent Muslim states did not renounce their vendetta against reason. They fought against the advances of Enlightenment philosophy and banned Western humanism as foreign and "imported," calling the intellectuals who studied it enemy agents and traitors to the nationalist cause. At the same time, they committed themselves to the massive importation of weapons from the West. The Arab states allocate a higher percentage of their gross domestic product to military expenditures than do the Western countries. This makes them doubly dependent, since Westerners use the income from arms sales to finance research and development and boost their aeronautic and space industries. A survey conducted by the International Labor Organization reveals that in the West employment in the arms industries is concentrated in the aeronautic and aerospace sectors: 33 percent in Belgium, 25 percent in France, 47 percent in Sweden, 27 percent in Italy, 35 percent in Finland and Greece, and 40 percent in the United States.[1] The supremacy of the West is not so much due to its military hardware as to the fact that its military bases are laboratories and its troops are brains, armies of researchers and engineers. The same survey shows that the arms industry provides an enormous number of jobs in other sectors, such as electronics and communications, which employ 20 percent of the manpower working in armaments in France, 23 percent in Sweden, 26 percent in Italy, and 30 percent in the United States.

The West creates its power through military research, which forces underdeveloped countries to become passive consumers. The weakness of the Arab nations stems from the fact that they buy weapons instead of choosing to do their own research. If it chose the latter course, an Arab state could pull off two miracles at one stroke: invest in an army of researchers and engineers, thus contributing to full employment, and free itself from military dependence on the West.

Middle Eastern states bought more than 40 percent of all arms sold throughout the world during the 1980s, wasting on hardware the wealth that could finance full employment:

> For the 1980–1983 period, all individual developing regions except the Middle East and Latin America had declining arms imports trends. The Middle East continues to be the major recipient of arms transfers. In 1983, its share of the world total reached almost 40% and thus its share of the developing countries total reached nearly 55%.[2]

Among the nine largest purchasers of arms in the world in 1983, four were Arab states: Iraq, Saudi Arabia, Libya, and Egypt.[3] What the officials of these states ignore is that the age of fetishism is over, and importing military hardware increases dependence. Power comes from the cultivation of the scientific spirit and participatory democracy. Despite its incredible investment in "King Khalid Military City," as the Americans call it, a megaproject that cost $6 billion, the Saudi regime was incapable of defending itself when the Gulf War broke out, and recourse to American help became inevitable.[4] The Gulf War exposed the extent of the military dependence of not just Saudi Arabia but all the Arab states. Arms purchases have blocked the creation of Arab intellectual and scientific power and its corollary, the diffusion via public education of democratic culture.

The problem of unemployment in the Arab world is structurally tied to the massive importation of arms, which burns up enormous state resources without creating a scientific infrastructure. I emphasize the issue of arms purchases because, as a woman, I consider that one of the most urgent questions which should be brought before the masses is, Do we really need to arm ourselves in such a stupid and sterile fashion? Wouldn't it be better to follow the example of Japan, which is highly developed precisely because it has not armed itself but has opted for power based on scientific research? The power of the modern West has been built by state propagation, through public schools, of that humanism that the Arab masses have never had the right to.

ABSENCE OF STATE SUPPORT AND THE REFORMERS' AMBIVALENT ATTITUDE

Secular humanism, as defined by the American sociologist James Davison Hunter, is one of the things taught by American public schools: "Public school curricula tend to reflect an emphasis on the individual as the measure of all things and on personal autonomy, feelings, personal needs, and subjectively derived values—all of which are independent of the transcendent standard implied in traditional theism."[5] American secular humanism was developed not so much against religion as against state interference in religion and especially manipulation of it. The success of this approach is demonstrated in the fact that the United States is one of the most religious countries imaginable; not only do churches still exist, but they are growing!

In addition to Protestant Christianity, which is omnipresent and constitutes the dominant religious culture, there are the other religious denominations: "About 28 percent of the U.S. population is Catholic; Jews make up about 2.5 percent. Mormons now constitute 1.6 percent of the population . . . and are one of the fastest growing denominations in America. Much more significant is the expansion of pluralism beyond the traditions of the Judeo-Christian faith. There are about as many Muslims in America, for example, as there are Mormons, and more Muslims than Episcopalians. The numbers of Hindus and Buddhists have also grown prodigiously since the end of World War II."[6] Preaching tolerance and freedom of thought, secular humanism is an attack not on God but on government officialdom and a ban on its use of government funds and institutions to propagate religion, any religion.

The majority of the colonized countries—that is, the non-Western countries—never experienced that phase of history so indispensable to the development of the scientific spirit, during which the state and its institutions became the means of transmitting the ideas of tolerance and respect for the individual. Above all else, colonial governments were brutal and culturally limited. The nationalist governments that supplanted them were just as brutal and just as hostile to the flowering of the scientific spirit and individual initiative. This produced a virtual cutoff of the Third World from the advances of humanism in the last centuries in both its aspects: the scientific aspect (promoting the use of government resources to invest in scientific research and encourage freedom to explore and invent), and the political aspect (establishing representative democracy, with citizens' exercise of the right to vote and to participate in political decision making). The result was the rampant malaise, which some call *'azma* (crisis), that now besets the colonized nations. In the modern Arab states it sometimes takes the form of intolerant outbursts and rejections of the present and our leaders. At other times it is expressed in the desire of lower-class young people to emigrate, to leave the Arab world to go to Europe. At still other times it can be seen in the world-weary attitude of the intellectual toward his own country, which Hichem Djait expresses so well:

> I feel humiliated to belong to a state with no outlook for the future nor ambition, a state that is authoritarian if not despotic, in which there is neither science, nor reason, nor beauty of life, nor real culture. This state holds me back; and in this provincial, ruralized society I feel smothered, as I suffer at being governed by uneducated and ignorant leaders. As an intellectual, I feel neurotic. It is human and legitimate that I project my malaise onto my society, but the popular revolts are testimony that this malaise is not just an intellectual construction.[7]

Djait speaks for the thousands if not millions who feel the same way. The tragedy is that Arabs, like the rest of the citizens of the Third World, have never had systematic access to the modern advances rooted in "the legacy of the Enlightenment, an ideological revolution that led to the debunking of medieval and reformational cosmologies and the undermining of feudal forms of political authority and theistic forms of moral authority."[8] But the break with the medieval state, which used the sacred to legitimize and mask arbitrary rule, never took place in the Arab world:

> The Muslims did not think of the phenomenon of modernity in terms of rupture with the past, but rather in terms of a renewed relation with the past. They didn't think about the phenomenon of modernity in terms of progress, but in terms of renaissance—thus, after all, in terms of magic or myth. In the majority of cases the Muslim approach, the approach of political and religious thinkers, was just the reverse of the principles implied by a correct understanding of Enlightenment thought.[9]

Today when we in the formerly colonized nations of the Arab world talk about democracy and the fear of democracy, we are speaking within a mental framework structured by lack, by truncations, by gaps. People experience modernity without understanding its foundations, its basic concepts. Freedom of thought is demonized and identified with Kharijite rebellion and disorder. The state uses the public schools to propagandize us. But the solution is not to supplant public schools with widespread privatization of education, as President Reagan proposed. The Arab world cannot count on help from the private sector, which doesn't recognize workers' rights and which, in the absence of any labor organizations or legislation mandating social insurance, systematically siphons off profits. The Arab private sector still does not contribute to the financing of social projects, and private education plays a small role in our culture. In the coming decades the state and its public schools will remain the only means of creating and propagating democratic culture and educating tolerant citizens.

The Moroccan philosopher ʿAli Umlil has devoted a whole book to the conceptual confusions that are the basis of "Arab reformism."[10] In it he shows that the nationalist movements at the end of the nineteenth and beginning of the twentieth centuries tried to modernize Muslim culture without breaking with the past, which was burdened with despotism and manipulation of the sacred. These movements introduced institutions and concepts of Western representative democracy like "constitution," "parliament," and "universal suffrage," while yet failing to educate the masses about the essential point: the sovereignty of the individual and freedom of opinion that are the philosophical basis of these institutions and concepts. The nationalists failed to think the problems through. Many were religious authorities forced to take part in the movement by military men and were inhibited by the barracks-room jingoism. We must not forget that the Arab world, like the rest of the Third World, saw the accession to power of the military in the 1950s and 1960s. The debate never became philosophical, as Umlil says: "The philosopher never counted; he was never invited to play the role of *daʿi,* propagandist for reformist ideas. That role went to the *fuqaha,* the religious authorities."[11]

Very quickly many reformers tried to link the concept of a constitution to the *shariʿa,* that is, to law of divine origin. The politicians, on the lookout for arguments to extend their authoritarianism, jumped at this opportunity to confuse the issue. Those who insisted on the distinction were condemned as infidels, blasphemers, allies of the colonizers, agents of the enemy.

Taha Husayn, one of our epoch's great defenders of the rationalist tradition who died in 1972, was harassed during his lifetime and judged and condemned after his death "as a manipulator of heathen, Hellenic ideas . . . a collaborator devoted to French thought and then in the service of American thought."[12] Anwar al-Jundi undertook to conduct a "trial" (*muhakama*) of Taha Husayn in a book of nearly four hundred pages published in 1984, in which Taha Husayn is refuted and called a *kafir.* The author of some of the most luminous pages ever penned on the life of the Prophet (which I was introduced to in primary school)[13], Taha Husayn is pictured on the cover of al-Jundi's book in the dock. In the Arab world at the end of the twentieth century we are seeing this lack of tolerance because probably al-Jundi and his like never had a primary school education in which they were taught that in a civilized society one does not prosecute an author who thinks differently. Al-Jundi's book is sold in bookstores that specialize in *al-thurat* (the heritage), and one can buy it for a few dirhams in Casablanca or Algiers. Apparently literature of this kind does not shock the officials of the Ministry of Information who are charged with censoring dangerous works. Intolerance is not dangerous. According to those in charge of information and culture in our era, it is books that challenge intolerance which are dangerous. The importation of a parliament and a constitution, without their essence being carefully explained, doesn't allow the masses to reflect calmly about a concept that until now has been tainted with sin: the concept of freedom (*al-hurriyya*). In our time, freedom in the Arab world is synonymous with disorder.

Freedom of religion (*al-hurriyya al-diniyya*) is freedom of belief and opinion, "with one sole condition: do not leave Islam." This is the way Rifaʿat al-Tahtawi, the most representative leader of the reform wing of the nationalist movement, defined one of the key concepts of the humanistic tradition, which is the basis of the parliamentary system.[14] Like the other reformers who helped design the modern Muslim state, he wanted a parliament and constitution with conditions attached to freedom of thought. Al-Tahtawi's ideas on tolerance were (and are) taught in primary and secondary school. He is the exemplary modernizing figure whose works are pompously taught as avant-garde texts that open new horizons for Arab youths. We start out in life thinking that *hurriyyat al-raʾy* (freedom of opinion) has limits and is closely supervised; there are *hudud* that must not be passed. It is understandable that many of us who have received such an education are confused and have difficulty understanding this century and what respecting another's opinion means.[15] The majority of the Arab people, who are still illiterate, are spared this kind of confusion; they never read al-Tahtawi in the original and never heard of the importance of *al-tasamuh* (tolerance).

Some Westerners are surprised to find that today university science departments and technological and scientific institutes are the breeding ground of fundamentalism; it is there that a large number of fundamentalists are recruited.[16] Actually, it is the most logical thing imaginable, considering the ambiguity that surrounds the

49

idea of freedom. How can scientists be trained in societies that reject freedom of thought as contrary to Islamic identity? Then there is the absence of the scientific infrastructure that only fundamental research can develop. The Arab states prefer to import finished technological products, especially arms, rather than train a powerful corps of scientists, which would risk destabilizing their authority from within. We therefore have a massive importation of products and a massive dispatch of students from the well-to-do class to Western universities. Letting the rest vegetate in a state of semiscience is no problem, even with the growth of fundamentalism in science departments that lack laboratories and adequate means for doing research.[17]

In this period of triumphant modernity, the Arab state (whether it is officially Islamic, like the monarchies, or socialist, like Syria and Algeria) has deprived us of our universal heritage of the last three centuries, and has disfigured the Muslim heritage through the teaching in its institutions. So let us return to the idea of fear of democracy and explore it a bit more.

THE AMBIGUITY OF FEAR: THE EMIR AND HIS CHAUFFEUR

"Fear" is a word that covers a gamut of different feelings: fear of slipping on the marble floor of an old *hammam* (bath) is not the same as dread of an approaching cyclone, and of course there is the very real fear of being arrested at dawn on a Friday and condemned at noon for a blasphemous text one wrote the night before.

This ambiguity which results from the extreme richness of the concept of fear, is also found in the word "democracy." The term covers an impressive array of freedoms and privileges, of rights to exercise and taxes to pay, from the right to eat pork or drink wine or read censored works; to the right to fall in love, have a platonic friendship or embark on an affair, marry one's partner or not, have children or not; to the right to demand a wage at least equal to the legal minimum wage, and appeal to a union if unjustly treated; to the right to elect a prime minister, and then to protest when the government-run television station gives him prime airtime at tax-payers' expense.

Associating democracy with fear certainly multiplies the ambiguities and increases the uncertainties. This is especially true if we remember that in a certain country—let us say Kuwait—the fear experienced by the emir is not the same as that felt by his wife and daughters. The emir's chauffeur—who is, let us say, a Palestinian—has different fears from his master's and also from those of the palace servants, who are likely to be Pakistani, North African, or Filipino. Each one, depending on his circumstances at the moment, feels and names the fears that beset him. That strange but omnipresent democracy is rather like the '*afrit* of the *Arabian Nights:* it can metamorphose into a ravishing young girl before the eyes of an amorous adolescent, or take the form of a winged dragon to terrify an official in charge of censorship. We are not trying to classify these fears, only to understand them a bit better—to go beyond stereotypes and, if we can, dissipate confusions about them.

IS DEMOCRACY MORE FOREIGN THAN THE AUTOMOBILE OR THE TELEPHONE?

Arabs have been discussing democracy for a century and a half. It came to them, paradoxically, in the baggage of the French and English colonial armies, the armies that brought other strange things, like the telephone, electricity, and the automobile. We don't have an Arabic word for democracy; we use the Greek word, *dimuqratiyya.* Two Arabs talking about democracy speak to each other in Greek, all the while remembering that the Greek heritage has been forbidden to them on the pretext that it is foreign. But we also have no words for telephone, electricity, and automobile. We call them by their foreign names, which we use and love, and there are no press reports of furious resistance to the automobile or electricity on Muslim soil. Although we always say *tumubil,* the word *siyara* exists, and the Arabic dictionaries have a list of other words to keep us from using those of "the enemy." But the masses prefer *tumubil,* and I have never heard a mechanic in Rabat say *siyara.* The same is true of the word for telephone. There is an Arabic word, *hatif*, but workers, peasants, and young people call it only *tilifun*. The dictionaries have created equivalents for "television," but everybody insists on buying a *tilivisiun*.

Despite their foreignness, the objects these words signify are coveted and voraciously consumed. Nowhere in the Muslim world is anyone challenging the use of these marvelous, indispensable little objects. In fact, the opposition movements, whatever cause they espouse, use them widely to push their propaganda. There is no political debate about their being foreign, and no political party, especially not the serious fundamentalists, are calling on us to choose between religion and the telephone. But this is the case with the notion of democracy. In the debate that rages today the traditionalists hold that one cannot be a Muslim and embrace *dimuqratiyya* at the same time, for that is foreign to Islamic culture. The regimes that draw their legitimacy from Islam (Saudi Arabia, for example) brand their opponents who advance the cause of democracy unbelievers, infidels. The irony is that in other Arab countries it is the opposition that impugns democracy as the constitutional foundation of the republic. This is the argument, for example, between the Algerian and Tunisian heads of state and their fundamentalist opposition.

It is thus not simply the foreign origin of democracy that makes it the center of controversy and conflict on the Muslim political chessboard. Apparently, unlike the automobile and the telephone, democracy is not perceived by all Muslims as being in their interests. Or rather, what those who reject it see in it does not seem to agree with their interests.

That makes the pertinent question to be asked, How is this fascinating democracy perceived? What is that *'afrita* (feminine gender), as it is called by Aunt 'Aziza, who finishes listening to the eight-thirty news every night (televised in classical Arabic) by murmuring, "But why does no one explain this *dimuqratiyya*? Is it a country or an *'afrita* or an animal or an island?" Afterward she goes to make her ablutions before turning toward the Ka'ba to say the evening prayer. Who perceives what democracy, and through what eyeglasses? Every Muslim, irrespective of sex, class, and income, can calculate immediately all the benefits they can draw from owning or at least using an automobile or a telephone. The faithful battle each other every day to have access to either of these objects. Although these products are manufactured mostly by multinational corporations that don't care a fig about Muslims and their interests, this insensitivity doesn't seem to disturb that same Muslim at all in his consumer enjoyment of these items.

It is not the same thing with democracy. Some groups of people think that it can promote their interests, especially those who know foreign languages, who have access to Western knowledge and culture (including such amenities as bank credit, social security, paid vacations, and so on). This is generally the case with bourgeois city dwellers, both men and women, who operate in the fields of finance and business. It is also the case with university professors, artists, and intellectuals, all of whom are involved in the creation and manipulation of knowledge, both traditional and modern. Others feel their interests to be terribly threatened by that *dimuqratiyya*. Considering the intensity of the opposition to democracy, which sometimes results in violence, they must believe that their very survival is in danger. This is apparently the situation of all those excluded from the good things mentioned above. Can it be that what they perceive of democracy is so distorted that its corollaries, personal and political initiative, seem threatening to them? Can it be that the most dispossessed in our societies cling to Islam because they fear being forgotten by their own people, who have found another identity and are involved in other networks, especially those very strong ones that create profit on an international scale?

But what is still more astonishing is that what goes for individuals goes for governments too. Some have more need of Islam, more need to find their identity in religion, than others. There are two kinds of governments: those that reject democracy as contrary to their identity, and those that embrace it. However, all of them use the automobile and the telephone and waste public funds on frivolous items that have no relation to the country's vital needs, like the arms that make us goggle-eyed when we hear the price and the obsolescent surveillance networks they buy to keep an eye on us.

53

But in the final analysis, these are just details. The essential point is that although all the Arab states are fond of electronic surveillance gadgets and sophisticated telecommunications systems, some of them nevertheless feel the need to base their political legitimacy on the past, while others feel no such need and embrace modernity. Why does Saudi Arabia, which moved heaven and earth during two U.S. administrations (those of President Carter and President Reagan) to buy the gem of American military electronics, the AWACS missile system, feel a stronger need to adhere to Islam than does Tunisia? What hides behind this outcry for religion that reverberates in the Arab world? What is its meaning to the person who expresses it—from the unemployed student of rural origin lost in the shantytowns of Cairo or Algiers, to the oil prince umbilically tied to the Pentagon? One thing is certain. The call for Islam in the 1990s expresses diverse needs that are not always archaic and are certainly not always of a spiritual nature.

As for the governments, there are some Muslim regimes that find their interests better protected if they base their legitimacy on cultural and symbolic grounds other than on democratic principles. The sacred, the past, ancestor worship seem to be the chosen grounds in most cases. This category groups together regimes as different as the kingdom of Saudi Arabia, the Iranian regime of Imam Khomeini or his caliph (successor), the military regime of Zia al-Haq in Pakistan, and the Sudanese regime that terrorizes its people in the name of the *shari'a*.

The same thing that is said about Muslim regimes can be said about the opposition forces. Most of the fundamentalist opposition movements root their struggle for liberation and progress in the past and reject the West and "its democracy." Other opposition forces claim Western democracy as the basis for dynamizing society and find in it no threat to their identity as Muslims or as Arabs:

> Who would be upset by a democratic state, or one aiming to be democratic, founded on a strong cultural identity both Arab and Islamic, boldly following the path of historical normality—that is, the path of modernity—but also the path of the other great poles of our future, some of which exist today and some of which will emerge?[18]

An Arab state open to the world and its ideas and enriched by the scientific and participatory heritage of recent centuries would be better able to defend our Arab and Islamic identity than the states that exist today. The Gulf War has clearly demonstrated that it is not the states of today, out of touch with the masses and their interests, frightened alike by rationalism and by the idea of democratic participation, that are able to protect Islam and the Muslims.

The Gulf War produced some very important revelations about emotional dynamics and people's sense of security. The Saudi and Kuwaiti officials were afraid of other Arabs, especially the Palestinians, and felt safer with their American colleagues. The war also proved that to have a chance at enjoying the wealth generated by oil, Arab youths must at least consider emigrating to the Western countries, to whose banks the petrodollars are automatically transferred. The war intensified the feeling of distrust, not to say hatred, between rich and poor which was already latent in the Arab world. This serious malaise, rooted in economic frustration and unequal opportunity, uses the language of religion as one of either protest and revolt or dissimulation and manipulation.

The mixture of frustration and religion is explosive for the whole Mediterranean area. We must be prepared to be crushed by its violence if we don't mobilize everyone of all nationalities to analyze it, understand it, and try to redress the bitterness and human degradation that it crystallizes. It is a malaise that affects both intellectuals and the masses. It creates a strong feeling of self-deprecation in young people and increases the mass emigration of the best educated as well as the most dispossessed to the West—a West that has responded by closing its borders and demanding visas for Arabs; that sees itself as owing them nothing, right after a war in which it proclaimed in the press that Middle Eastern oil was essential to its economy. The dream of happiness for many Arabs, from unemployed youths to rich industrialists, is a European vacation. Many take the step, trying frantically to leave, but find the need for travel visas barring the way at all turns. Our nation, frustrated in its desire for full employment and political responsibility, is becoming a huge land of individuals who roam standing in place, one eye on the television and the other on their passports. *ʿAzma* is the story heard everywhere.

THE GREAT MALAISE: *ʿAZMA* (CRISIS) AND *DAYAʿ* (WASTE)

When I visit a Muslim country, whether Pakistan or Egypt or Algeria, what strikes me as a sociologist is first of all the strong feeling of bitterness in the people—the intellectuals, the young, peasants. I see bitterness over blocked ambition, over frustrated desires for consumption—of clothes, commodities, and gadgets, but also of cultural products like books and quality films and performances which give meaning to life and reconcile the individual with his environment and his century. In no Western country have I ever seen such intense bitterness over wasted talent, spoiled chances, inequality of opportunity, or absurd career blockage. What always surprises me in the United States, for example, is that even people with the most mediocre talent seem to find a way to use the few gifts that nature has given them. In our country what is unbearable, especially when you listen to the young men and women of the poor class, is the awful waste of talent. "*Ana dayaʿ*" ("My life is a mess") is a leitmotiv that one hears constantly. I don't find this sense of failure which people drag around with them in any European city. For me the absence of moaning and groaning is a sign that I am on foreign territory, where talent follows a "relatively" normal course to emerge, struggle, expand, and flower.[19]

To my mind, this mourning over wasted talent must be taken into consideration if one is to understand how the "Muslims," and particularly the lower-class youth, who are sorely threatened by high unemployment, mobilize around the opposition between Islam and democracy. Their attachment to this movement is in fact a cry for the opportunity to benefit from the culture of this century and its valorizing skills. But how, I will be asked, can a young person threatened with unemployment oppose democracy and prefer religion as the basis of his struggle to get on in the world? Religion doesn't create more jobs, after all. But what it does is create a space for renewal and reflection on the universe and its injustices.

MINA DOESN'T UNDERSTAND UNIONS, BUT SHE UNDERSTANDS INJUSTICE

An interview I had with Mina, a Moroccan carpet weaver who was hospitalized with a broken wrist incurred in an on-the-job accident, perfectly summarizes the democratic, cultural, and linguistic handicaps suffered by people like her. As a result of her accident, and despite ten years' seniority, Mina had been fired by the factory where she worked, which offered her no medical coverage or compensation. When during a visit to the hospital in Rabat I urged her to take her case to the labor inspector, she reacted violently. I had apparently touched a sore point. "Listen, Fatima, just because you are educated and I am illiterate, you have no right to treat me like an idiot. You tell me to go see the labor inspector as if I had not thought of it; you tell me to go to the labor union as if I had not thought of it! I tell you that Allah is my defender; he is my union and my inspector!"

Choking with rage about the situation, she tore off the scarf that modestly covered her hair and threw it on the floor in a traditional gesture of extreme agitation. She raised her eyes toward the sky, framed in the little window of her room, and cried, "Allah, you who know all about this *zulm* [injustice], I want you to burn down the factory and crush the boss to bits! Allah, do you hear me? 'And when My servants question thee concerning Me, then surely I am nigh.' They told me that you hear the *mazlum* [the one who is wronged]! Where are you, Allah? I need you in this country of monsters!"[20]

Meanwhile the nurses were rushing into the room and urging me to leave. But Mina shouted, "Let her alone, let us alone! I am opening my heart! Let me cry! Don't tell me to shut up or I will add you to the list of the boss and the union!" The door was softly closed; everyone is afraid of someone who in such a state of anger and pain invokes the divine.

Mina continued to pour out her heart: "Fatima, listen carefully to the details, which you don't know about. I worked ten years without a labor card, without a contract. My name never appeared on any payroll. I was hired every day to work in the factory as if it were the first day. The first year I went with 'A'isha to talk to the union; an iron bar from the loom had fallen on us. 'A'isha, who is older than I, had more experience. The union sent us to the labor inspector. And do you know what the labor inspector did? He tattled to the boss instead of defending us! The next day the boss called us in: 'So, you whores, you went to the labor inspector? You betrayed me and washed our dirty linen in public. You could have come and politely asked me to buy you some medicine. Ungrateful monsters! You are fired!' We didn't find work for six months. Our names had been reported to all the other factories in the area."

Mina, like millions of others who live a daily life of frustrated desires, is not a fatalist. A fatalist doesn't explode in anger and curse the boss. This is where Islam plays a key role in the struggle to preserve dignity. Having God as one's defender when the boss, the union, the labor inspector violate one's rights probably doesn't change things in the short run. But meanwhile, the fired and exploited worker can go to the great palace that never closes its doors: the palace of our symbolic heritage. Mina was fired and left without rights and without money, but she had not forfeited her humanity; she could talk to Heaven and its Master. Islam gives someone like Mina a framework within which to express her pain and to change it into anger and a program for vengeance.

But here we run up against the limits of the traditional symbolic heritage, which doesn't make it possible for her to conceive of a world where she would have the right to medical coverage and social security, or even less to participate in such a world. For that to happen the imam, the Muslim head of state, would have to invest part of the government's funds in modern institutions that would permit citizens like Mina to enjoy their rights and force the private sector to cooperate in giving them their rights. Arab industrialists are only "competitive" in the European market because they engage in unregulated capitalism that more or less deprives workers of their rights and gives them no protection. Like the government, Arab businessmen fear democracy and the possibility that their workers might be transformed into responsible citizens who demand their rights. Like the oil princes, they are ready to invest in all the religions of the world if that would block the encroachment of democracy. One of the reasons for unemployment among young university graduates in Morocco is that the factory owner fears letting in among his workers "educated" people who have participated in demonstrations on their campuses. During an investigation in 1987 into the role of women in the textile industry, many workers testified that it was much easier to be hired if one wore a traditional djellaba: "If you wear jeans and a T-shirt you have to wait for hours, and after the interview they tell you that you are not qualified." Mina has no idea of the modern democratic mechanisms that could change the factory without burning it down. Her outcry, her choice of words, show that only the tradition of democratic rebellion is alive and well. Challenging the boss is the only available possibility, and also, alas, the last resort.[21]

One part of the world draws all its programs and references only from its symbolic and civilizational heritage: the traditional heritage. It is important to be acquainted, even superficially, with this program, since we are called on to live in a world that is more crowded and interconnected than ever. Despite its extreme politicization and all the financial and administrative manipulations it is subjected to, the Islamic heritage continues to have an extraordinary richness. It expresses the hope of the faithful and offers them two essential things: a sense of identity and the power to struggle.

Muslims today live under the surveillance of non-Muslim satellites that can, if need be and as the Gulf War proved, serve rapacious interests and aim their missiles at civilian populations. As the sole symbolic heritage of millions of the disinherited, Islam is called on to play an important role as their identifying referent, while they await their entry into the field of modern knowledge. This is what makes it necessary for us to examine the two fundamental texts that today confront each other in the conflict between Islam and democracy: the United Nations Charter and the Koran.

4

The United Nations Charter

When we speak about the conflict between Islam and democracy, we are in fact talking about an eminently legal conflict. If the basic reference for Islam is the Koran, for democracy it is effectively the United Nations Charter, which is above all a superlaw.

The majority of Muslim states have signed this covenant, and thus find themselves ruled by two contradictory laws. One law gives citizens freedom of thought, while the *sharic̣a,* in its official interpretation based on *tac̣a* (obedience), condemns it. Most Muslims, who are familiar with the Koran from very early in life, have never had occasion to read the United Nations Charter or to become acquainted with its key concepts. For many people, the charter is like the Haguza monster of my childhood: you hear about it, but no one has ever yet seen it. It has come onto our shores mysteriously folded away in the attaché cases of diplomats and, like a harem courtesan, has never succeeded in getting out. With age and confinement it has become, like Haguza, the more terrifying because of its invisibility.

But first I must introduce Haguza.

HAGUZA, THE MONSTER OUT OF THE NORTH

I was born in one of the last harems of Fez in the 1940s, just before the walls of that honorable institution began to crack under the force of modernity. I had what is called a happy childhood, living in a house that had an enormous traditional courtyard floored with black and white marble, making a gigantic design for endless games of hopscotch. Four stairways, one in each of the four corners, pushed their green faience way upward, like magic columns, to one of the highest terraces in the medina of Fez. Ten cousins of the same age, both boys and girls, were constantly running around, laughing and playing games. For sure, it was a catastrophe for the adults. Siesta time in the Mernissi household was impossible. Guests always begged leave to depart before lunch. Our mothers had to shout to make themselves heard—until the day an aunt came from Tétouan, a city in the north that was a center for Muslims chased out of Andalusia. She brought with her a terrifying legend that she probably inherited from her Spanish ancestors: the legend of Lalla Haguza.

Haguza comes once a year on a special holiday for which people prepare a ritual dish of rather thick couscous with milk. Haguza hides behind the shadowy staircase and watches for the child who makes any noise, ripping that child open if its mother does not intercede in time and say the required prayers. Suddenly the great mansion becomes silent, and the childish population is divided (as are Arabs today on the question of democracy) into two camps: those who want to encounter Haguza, and those whose jaws are locked with fear. I was of course in the second group. I wouldn't go near the stairs, even in daylight, except when holding on to my mother's caftan. The daredevil group, on the contrary, led by my cousin Ahmad, was all for meeting her. Very early in the morning we had to be at our posts before the monstrous Haguza occupied the stairway; armed with slingshots, we would lay her low. Once she was brought down, we would negotiate the right of way.

The legend of Lalla Haguza enlivened a great part of our childhood. Then one day we stumbled into puberty and found that our adolescence coincided with the struggle for national independence. All of us, men and women, rushed headlong into the streets of the medina to chant "*Al-hurriyya jihadiuna hatta narha*" ("We will fight for freedom until we get it"). Fear took flight, and everything was possible; the Arab world opened up like a flower giddy with its own perfume. The future had the color of the Moroccan sky, that unparalleled, extraordinary, and so persistent blue. Haguza became

61

the code word for everything we didn't know and that was frightening. Sometimes in the lively youth meetings of the Istiqlal (Independence) party, which drew hundreds of men and women from all corners of the medina, Ahmad would poke me in the ribs and say "*Haguza ma'ana*" ("Haguza is with us").

The United Nations Charter is a little like Haguza: neither seen nor known, and resembling everything bizarre. It will remain like Haguza, until the day it leaves the briefcases of our diplomats and enters the public schools and the suqs. Until that day this venerable charter, like a kidnaped virgin, will be jealously guarded by those who have signed it.

THE WELL-GUARDED SECRET OF SAN FRANCISCO

The United Nations Charter has the effect of law in the territory of the Muslim countries that are members of the United Nations and signatories of the charter. And what a body of law it is! It is impossible to imagine one more forceful, for it claims to be superior to all local laws, the ideal that will reform and transform them. It is the supreme model: a higher law than those of the states' constitutions themselves. The preamble to the United Nations Universal Declaration of Human Rights declares:

> Now, therefore, The General Assembly proclaims This Universal Declaration of Human Rights as a common standard of achievement for all peoples and all nations, to the end that every individual and every organ of society, keeping this Declaration constantly in mind, shall strive by teaching and education to promote respect for these rights and freedoms and by progressive measures, national and international, to secure their universal and effective recognition and observance, both among the peoples of Member States themselves and among the peoples of territories under their jurisdiction.

The charter was signed in San Francisco on June 26, 1945. Several Muslim states were among the original members of the United Nations: Iran, Turkey, Lebanon, Egypt, Syria, and Saudi Arabia.

The others hastily sent diplomats to add signatures on their behalf. Soon afterward the United Nations established conditions of admission for new members which obliged them to sign documents in which they recognized the charter as superior to their national constitutions. Since most Muslim states had just emerged from decades of colonial occupation, they were ready to do anything in order to sit side by side as partners with their ex-colonizers. They must have read the text of General Assembly Resolution 116 of November 21, 1947, which provides that

> any state which desires to become a Member of the United Nations shall submit an application to the Secretary-General. This application shall contain a declaration, made in a formal instrument, that it accepts the obligations contained in the Charter. . . . If the application is approved, membership will become effective on the date on which the General Assembly takes its decision on the application.

So it was that after World War II there appeared on Muslim territory regimes that were parliamentary democracies on paper and that introduced laws different from the Islamic rule of *ta'a* which these states had chosen to identify themselves with and from which *ra'y* (personal opinion) and reason were banished, especially the explosive Article 18 of the Universal Declaration of Human Rights, which said in part:

> Everyone shall have the right to freedom of thought, conscience and religion. *This right shall include freedom to have or to adopt a religion or belief* of his choice, either individually or in community with others and in public or private [emphasis added]. . . .

The Universal Declaration of Human Rights, adopted by the General Assembly on December 10, 1948, as "a common standard of achievement for all peoples and all nations," should have initiated a debate about freedom of thought and the relationship between religion and the state. The face of the Muslim world would have been changed if after 1948 Saudi Arabia, one of the original

63

signatories of the United Nations Charter, had mobilized its huge education and propaganda establishment and its banking network to explain to the people that the secular state provided for in Article 18 is not so much one staffed by *mulhid* (atheistic) officials as one that prohibits its agents from squandering public funds to push their interpretation of religion.

The states that were signatories of the charter and the international conventions had a choice between two possible approaches: they could seize the opportunity of the adoption of these new universal laws to open up a full public debate on the nature of power and explain to the people the mechanisms of participatory democracy; or they could hide these laws away, sequestering them like clandestine courtesans who are an embarrassment when one wants to play the role of imam and demand *ta'a*. It was the second option that was chosen. Hiding these laws, putting them behind a *hijab,* became the strategy and the objective. Mobilizing the media and millions of teachers to explain Article 18 would have meant explaining the philosophical basis of the secular state. It would have required banning the use of the government apparatus to publicize *ta'a,* blind obedience to the president of the republic.

If the Arab states had chosen the way of representative democracy, we would not have witnessed one of the miracles of the century—"reigns" of presidents of Arab republics as long as those of kings. The Arab world is probably one of the rare regions of the world where a presidency can last a lifetime. Habib Bourguiba of Tunisia, for example, agreed to step down only under pressure. As for Hafaz al-Assad of Syria, he has just announced his fourth term. The long reign of President Bourguiba, like the four terms of President Assad, is not subject to the routine procedures of representative democracy, which would reflect the whims of very changeable public opinion. The long tenure in office of Arab presidents can be explained in only two ways: it is the result of either supernatural forces (divine grace or magic) or much more mundane acts, like rigging the vote. President Bourguiba, whom we all admire for his past as a nationalist leader, would certainly have had a shorter presidency if he had not put government funds into publicity for himself as the *mujahid akhbar* (Great Warrior). If I mention President Bourguiba, it is because Tunisia is one of the rare Arab states that have declared themselves modern—by contrast with Morocco, where tradition is unequivocally embraced.

If we are to sharpen our understanding of the intimate link between authoritarianism and the state's refusal to engage the masses in the great debate that modern life demands of us—that is, the question of the secular state—we have to understand how the system operates. The regime of President Bourguiba monopolized the mass media and the schools to tell citizens that they must modernize and renounce tradition while refusing to grant them the essence of modernity: freedom of thought and participation in decision making. The government lauded democracy while robbing the Tunisian citizens of the right to have a say in how their tax money was spent. The result was that Arab countries like Tunisia which call themselves liberal, or those like Algeria which call themselves socialist, created the most confusion among their peoples and thus brought on the fundamentalist opposition that now threatens them.

The fundamentalists' argument is that if Islam is separated from the state, no one will any longer believe in Allah and the memory of the Prophet will dim. Since we are constantly bombarded via satellite by advertisements for all sorts of products, from soap to films, the state must defend Islam. Such reasoning is in fact an insult to Islam, with its suggestion that Islam can succeed only if it is imposed on people in a totalitarian manner, through courts that punish those who drink wine or refuse to fast during Ramadan. According to this argument, Islam has nothing to offer a modern citizen, who would quickly abandon it if state surveillance were lifted. We shall see in the following chapters that Islam has much to offer. As both Christianity and Judaism have done, Islam can not only survive but thrive in a secular state. Once dissociated from coercive power, it will witness a renewal of spirituality. Christianity and Judaism strongly rooted in people's hearts are what I have seen in the United States, France, and Germany. In those countries the secular state has not killed religion; rather, it has put a brake on the state's manipulation of religion. It took three centuries of effort by many European philosophers and several revolutions for this fundamental nuance to be developed, accepted, and made understandable to the masses.

The Muslim states, which since independence have controlled the networks of propaganda and mass education, have never put these networks in the service of that new idea of the secular state which Article 18 formulates so simply. By clearly affirming the right to freedom of belief, Article 18 directly challenges the right of a state to use violence against citizens and makes the principle of tolerance inviolable. However, the Muslim leaders who signed the United Nations Charter and the conventions that have accumulated over half a century are scarcely tolerant. They have not only increased measures to mask all conflict between the charter and their authoritarian interpretation of Islam; they have also used their national budgets to betray the charter and forbid as contrary to Islam the freedom of thought which it proclaims, and to preclude citizens from becoming familiar with its rules and regulations through regular democratic participation.

THE MASQUERADE OF RESERVATIONS

The Muslim states have used numerous amendments and reservations to the charter and its conventions to plug up the cracks that might have allowed citizens to breathe a bit of freedom or gain some small experience of equality. An Arab woman can only laugh at the amendments of the Egyptian Republic to Article 16 of the Convention on the Elimination of All Forms of Discrimination Against Women (December 8, 1979), signed by the pharaonic diplomats on July 16, 1980. Listen to the double-talk that these venerable officials presented as a "reservation," and you will understand why the United Nations is seen by the masses as a charade:

> Reservation to the text of article 16 concerning the equality of men and women in all matters relating to marriage and family relations during the marriage and upon its dissolution, without prejudice to the Islamic Sharia's provisions whereby women are accorded rights equivalent to those of their spouses so as to assure a just balance between them. This is out of respect for the sacrosanct nature of the firm religious beliefs which govern marital relations in Egypt and which may not

66

be called in question and in view of the fact that one of the most important bases of these relations is an equivalency of rights and duties so as to ensure complementarity which guarantees true equality between the spouses.[1]

What do we understand from reading the text of this reservation? Not much, since the equality ensured in Article 16 in no way "prejudices" the *sharia* if that is interpreted to guarantee a "just balance." It is precisely this lack of clarity which characterizes the modern Arab state and which has led to confusion and the fundamentalist violence that we know today.

In fact the text reveals the symptoms of the grave malady the Arab states suffer from, which they hush up as shameful: their visceral rejection of the principle of equality. But they can't admit this at the diplomatic level without being condemned as primitive and savage. On the other hand, stating that the *sharia* does not promote equality would risk having to make a choice between it and the charter and calling the principles of the United Nations into question. Only the delegates of those nations that have signed the conventions declaring equality and freedom to be the bases of their political system can be seated in the United Nations. So where is the loophole that permits an Arab state with its "reservations" and "amendments" to produce two miracles: to be seated in the United Nations as a signatory of all the conventions, while its officials manipulate the texts to make restrictive interpretations of principles that don't admit of restriction—equality and freedom?

This reveals the role that religion plays in the subtle drama that our heads of state stage: they must present a modern face at the United Nations in New York, and the face of an Abbasid caliph to terrorize us at home. The "amendments" and "reservations" will multiply to camouflage all the legal texts that come into conflict with *taʿa* and affirm the right to *raʾy*.[2] For the Arab countries the United Nations, with its charter and its conventions, is an arena for manipulation and hypocrisy.[3] This opinion was only reinforced, alas, by the Gulf War, in which the noble principles of the charter and the lofty ideal of universality and responsibility acted to legitimize the use of force. But the fact is that the Arab states have not been using their media and educational networks to inform and educate their citizens about the revolutionary content of the charter, which they condemn to a semiclandestine existence.

TV ISLAM

The principles of the charter will never take root in modern Arab consciousness. Today the opposition leaders, who preach their discontent in terms of sacred concepts like *zulm* (injustice) and *ʿadala* (justice) and attract to the mosques youths worried by the specter of unemployment, with reason brand democracy and the charter as foreign. Most of them have never had a chance to hear anyone explain on the radio or television the universal application of that new law from San Francisco.

Religious programs produced by imam-officials and American films filled the Arab radios and television screens during the 1980s, years that saw the Islamic challenge intensify.[4] In 1987 almost a fifth, 18.6 percent, of the radio programs in Egypt were devoted to religious programs, and only 14.7 percent were cultural programs out of a total of 56,455 broadcasting hours a year. Israel, where religion plays a central role in society, devotes only 0.8 percent of its 34,281 broadcasting hours a year to religion, and 8.9 percent of broadcasting time was given to cultural programs during the same period. In socialist Algeria in 1985 the radio time accorded to religious programs (1,434 hours) was almost double that given to cultural programs (867 hours). The remainder of the 19,981 annual radio hours was devoted to sports and entertainment. But it is Saudi Arabia that apparently has the greatest fear for the faith of its citizens; 30 percent of its radio programs (a total of 36,865 hours) are devoted to religion. Even Catholic Italy, which has the honor of protecting the pope's infallibility in the sumptuous Vatican, does not accord so many hours to religious programs, but rather devotes 37 percent of its programs to culture.

Never have we in the Arab states, even in the programs called educational by UNESCO statisticians, been exposed to long dissertations on the United Nations Charter, that superlaw that we are told threatens our cultural integrity. Television might have been an ideal instrument for explaining exactly how we are being threatened. Arab leaders could not say that the United Nations Charter was banned from Arab television because it was foreign. Our very Arab television gives us Hollywood films (although they tend to be films that don't cost much, like silent movies and films from Hollywood's classic era).

The greatest consumers of American films are the oil states. Although Egypt has its own film industry, it imports 38.7 percent of its films from the United States. According to UNESCO, socialist Algeria imports 60 percent of its films from the West. But when we look at the figures more closely, we see that the West that fascinates the Algerian decision makers doesn't emanate from Russia. It is the United States that dominates the imagination of the average Algerian, since a third of the imported films were American. Even Arab leaders who opt for the "defunct socialist way" don't allow too much talk about socialist principles, because people might stumble onto little anomalies like the "dictatorship of the proletariat" and the place of honor that should be given to the avant-garde. A study of Arab socialism as it is broadcast and televised has yet to be done. It might give us a needed good laugh.

I think that in Iraq and Syria, other Arab countries that opted for socialist-style modernity, the officials who regulate television had no trouble disguising Papa Marx as a despotic caliph. Turning Marx into a monster was not an arduous task in Damascus (the former Umayyad capital) or Baghdad (the Abbasid capital). From the moment that the key concept of "dictatorship" was given a sacred hue and made honorable, even if it was a dictatorship of the proletariat, the memory of the caliphs could be renewed and find new life. In the 1980s Amnesty International reports listed several Arab socialist countries as sites of torture and killing.[5] The Arab avant-garde was carefully muzzled and its rowdiest members sent off, willingly or unwillingly, to London and Paris.[6] As for the "proletariat," which might have raised the ancient Kharijite specter in the shantytown powder kegs full of partially employed youths who never succeeded in entering the modern sector that socialism extolled, it made only brief appearances on television, sandwiched between football games and religious programs.

We had to wait for the launching of private associations at the end of the 1980s to see human rights come into the streets of the

Arab capitals and to begin to see translations of and commentaries on international charters and agreements circulate in Arabic for a few dirhams. The literate masses pounced on these brochures to read about what *hurriyyat al-raʾy* (freedom of opinion) meant and about how the United Nations Charter could protect them against torture.[7] It was only through the efforts of intellectuals of the Left and university students, agitating for rights of the individual, that bulky translations of Amnesty International documents began to circulate in Arabic. These groups were also instrumental in seeing that whole passages from these documents were printed in the leftist press when leaders came out of prison or succeeded in resuming activity after being tried and fined.

When one hears André Glucksmann, one of the intellectuals who influence Western opinion, reduce Muslim fundamentalism to the people's lack of understanding of "the difficulties of the modern state" and to their desire to "[smash] that provocative Western window that is Israel," one is sorry to have to say that Glucksmann's ignorance of "the Muslims" exceeds the ignorance he attributes to them. His is the arrogant conviction that he alone has the truth, and the other is afflicted with an atavistic inability to understand. Moreover, his saying that fundamentalism "can be destroyed only from within" is to claim that the people meekly submit to fundamentalist authoritarianism without a struggle, while exonerating himself as a Westerner from his responsibility in the matter.[8] The Muslim masses battle every day against intolerance and authoritarianism. Glucksmann's remarks are also a way of saying that we make no effort to be informed, although to be sure the Amnesty International reports are very short, allotting two or three pages to each country. Just leaf through the report for 1989. On page 282 it says that in Iraq torture is frequently inflicted on political prisoners, the "disappearance" of a large number of persons has been reported, and hundreds of executions have taken place. Turn to page 274. There the report notes the arrest of presumed opponents of the monarchy in Saudi Arabia in 1988, especially in the Eastern Province, as well as of pilgrims participating in the hajj, the Muslims' annual pilgrimage. At least twenty-six death sentences were followed by execution, and punishment by amputation was applied.

Saying that the masses do not struggle blurs the picture by simplifying a complex reality. At the very least it is necessary when the word "fundamentalism" is thrown around to distinguish between two types: government fundamentalism, the official culture that serves as a barrier against democratic education, and opposition fundamentalism. Above all it is essential to avoid putting all Muslims in the same bag, thus denying the existence of the social distinctions that are found when Europeans are spoken of: governing class, intellectuals, and masses. Each of these groups has its own interests and expresses them in a loaded political situation that forces it to decide between two equally dangerous, disabling choices: belief versus atheism, and obedience versus freedom.

The cultural void created by the nonuse of the government mass media to explain the charter and the international agreements, combined with massive doses of religious programming and faking of the parliamentary game and manipulation of the vote, have plunged the Arab masses into a state of confusion and intolerance. Let us look at the unfortunate result when the title "president of the republic" is translated into the Arabic language.

"IMAMIZATION" OF THE PRESIDENCY: RA'IS AL-JUMHURIYYA

The least confused Muslims are those whose heads of state have chosen to keep their traditional titles. In the absence of a proper education in civics, they don't have to do somersaults to accommodate *ra'is* (head) as a translation of "president." Those who live in a monarchy, as I do, have the least problem with official titles. The word *malik* (king) poses no difficulty because it is not new; it exists in the Koran and in the dictionaries of medieval Arabic. We have whole treatises dealing with *mulk* (earthly power), its nature, its rituals, and its requirements. *Ra'is al-jumhuriyya* (president of the republic), however, is not part of our heritage. It does not exist in the Koran or in the old dictionaries. In the dictionary *Lisan al-ʿArab* (Language of the Arabs) the two words *ra'is* and *jumhur* exist, but they are unconnected. When they are combined the result is a bizarre cocktail in which neither François Mitterrand nor George

71

Bush would recognize himself, for what emerges has more to do with an Abbasid imam than anything else.

The word "republic" refers to a form of government in which power is not held by a single individual and in which the headship of state (the presidency) is not a hereditary post. This word does not exist in the Koran, although the words *hizb* (party) and *haqq* (right) are found there.

The *Lisan al-ʿArab* tells us that the word *al-jumhur*, which is the root of *jumhuriyya*, means "the majority of the people," but also the most noble of them. Nevertheless, the key idea is of grouping and gathering together. The verb *jamhara* means "gathering together," explains Ibn Manzur, the author of the dictionary. He gives several examples that affirm this gregarious and almost standardizing dimension of *jumhur*, pointing to a link in Arabic which relates to the horde, whereas the Latin *res publica* defines the nature of the leader's power by implicitly emphasizing the border between the public and the private. One of the examples the dictionary gives to help us understand the meaning of the word is "*jumhuriyya* wine": "A wine that makes one very drunk"; it is called *jumhuriyya* because "most people consume it." So we conclude that *jumhuriyya* describes a certain consensus, a unity within the collectivity; the word says nothing about the limits of the power exercised by the leader.

And how is the word "president" translated into Arabic? "To preside," from the Latin *praesidere,* means "to occupy the place of authority (as in an assembly) . . . to direct, control, or regulate proceedings as chief officer," says *Webster's Third New International Dictionary.* However, in passing from English derived from Latin to Arabic, "president of the republic" becomes *raʾis al-jumhuriyya,* and in this transition from one semantic system to another the functions and position are so changed that the concept is scarcely recognizable. The head, *raʾis,* commands the rest of the body; I cannot lift my little finger if my brain doesn't send the necessary signal. In moving from Latin to Arabic the idea of the assembly disappears; instead there is a dramatic focus on the highest point, the head. One passes from a spatial vision of presidency, which is exercised according to a horizontal schema (directing from the front of an assembly) to an Arabic bodily schema, which establishes a vertical

72

relationship between leader and led, and in which what presides is the brain, while the others stupidly follow.

According to the *Lisan al-ʿArab, raʾis* is "the highest point of everything." That is the most common meaning the word has in the Koran, where it occurs about eighteen times.[9] *Raʾasa,* the dictionary tells us, means "to strike someone on the head." Here we are far indeed from a relationship of peaceful exchange between leader and led. Ibn Manzur wants to make sure that we have understood clearly: "*Raʾasa . . .* means to give orders to people." The *raʾis* is "master of the people." On the off chance that we have not grasped the violence embedded in the relationship with the leader, he adds that "the original meaning of *irtaʾasa* is to take someone by the neck and make him lower his head to the ground."

An Arab who says "president of the republic" thus doesn't imagine an assembly in which a *raʾis* is seated facing those to whom he is supposed to listen in order to allow them to debate. When I, as an Arab woman, say *raʾis al-jumhuriyya,* I imagine a head on a body, and then I try to place myself as best I can in that bodily picture, which inevitably condemns me to powerlessness. I try to nestle down in the left toe or some obscure nook like that.

The Universal Declaration of Human Rights certainly represents a traumatic break with medieval mental schemas. Its concepts, anchored in Enlightenment philosophy, could have emerged and changed perceptions in societies with a despotic tradition only if a systematic program of education and civic training had been undertaken. Such education would have been successful in transforming attitudes in depth if it had been carried out on two levels: with continual training and real participation, through the vote and representation, in democratic arrangements for decision making. Unless they are minutely remodeled, concepts of power and its use shaped in the Arabic language, which has been tightly controlled since the Abbasids so that it could not diverge from its caliphal past, swallow up all reference to the plurality that is the basis of democracy. It is in light of this lack in modern civic society, which is supposed to permit the Muslim masses access to modern humanism, that we must now return to the Koran, the basic text of Islam. In the chapters that follow we will learn why ambitious modern youths, aspiring to realize their talents and to live

73

with dignity, are finding in the Koran concepts that express their insecurities. Written Islam, the *risala* (message), is a vast domain that resounds with a music that has the wings of hope. But to hear this murmur, we must stay away from the television mosques where the imams paid by oil money hold forth. Above all we must concentrate on ourselves, as our Sufi ancestors did long ago, in search of the Simorgh, that fabulous creature well buried in the only place able to contain it—deep within ourselves.

5

The Koran

The Koran is a book divided into 114 suras of varying length, from
a few lines to several pages. According to Imam Ibn Kathir, there
are 6,000 verses in the Koran, 77,439 words, and not less than
321,180 letters.[1] It was revealed orally in the Arabic language by
Allah to the Prophet Muhammad with the angel Gabriel as intermediary.[2]

The Prophet was forty years old when God advised him of his
mission. The angel Gabriel visited him on Saturday night, then on
Sunday night, and on Monday he revealed to him that he had been
chosen by God to be the Prophet to receive the *risala,* the revealed
message. This was in A.D. 610 at Hira, a place of retreat near Mecca
where Muhammad used to go to meditate.[3] The first verses revealed to him were an order to be informed and to learn:

1. Read: in the name of thy Lord who createth,
2. Createth men from a clot.
3. Read: And thy Lord is the Most Bounteous,
4. Who teacheth by the pen,
5. Teacheth man that which he knew not. (sura 96)

The revelations succeeded one another from time to time over a
period of more than twenty years, from 610 to 632, the date of the
Prophet's death.[4] The last verse is supposed to have been revealed
to him nine days before his death.[5] But he didn't begin to preach at
once; because Mecca, his native city, was hostile to him, he kept

his mission secret for three years. He received Allah's order to begin to preach publicly only in 613, and he continued preaching for ten years, until 622, when the hostility of the city put his life and that of his Companions in danger. He then decided to migrate to Medina.[6] He was fifty-three years old, and that year was declared the first of the Muslim calendar, which begins with the Hejira (migration), referring to the exodus of the Muslim community. According to al-Suyuti, at the time of his departure the Prophet had received eighty suras, which are called the Meccan suras; the remaining thirty-four, the Medinan suras, were revealed to him during the ten years he lived in Medina.[7] Opinions differ as to the place of revelation of the suras; by Ibn Kathir's account, the Prophet received twenty-five suras in Medina, and so eighty-nine in Mecca.[8]

The order of the written Koran was decided on just after the Prophet's death, according to some sources; others maintain that it was put together by six people during the Prophet's lifetime; and still others hold that it was done during the reign of caliph ʿUmar, who acceded to power in 13/634.[9] What is certain is that the community very quickly realized the importance of putting the revelations into writing to avoid the danger of forgetting, despite the existence of Companions who had a marvelous facility for faultless memorization. The official version we have today was collected and written down during the reign of the third caliph, ʿUthman (23–35/644–55).[10] This ʿUthmani version is accepted by all Muslims, Sunni and Shiʿite alike, as the holy book, unique and unifying, the words with which Allah has honored human beings by showing them the way to peace and prosperity on earth and Paradise in the Beyond. This unanimous acceptance, as can be imagined, is one of the secrets of the power of the text and its hold on the generations that have transmitted it as is for fifteen centuries.

One of the extremist Kharijite sects refused to include sura 12, entitled "Joseph," on the grounds that "a love story is not permitted in the Koran."[11] This sect was and still is considered bizarre and highly irresponsible. It was called the ʿAjradi sect after the name of its leader, ʿAjarrad, who took other very unusual positions: for example, that of his aversion to children. Those who were not born

Muslim were regarded as destined for hell; those born Muslim had to be kept apart from the community until they were invited to embrace Islam formally.[12] The least we can say about the ʿAjradi is that they were rather strange. Daring to reject a Koranic verse, a fortiori a sura, throws discredit on the one who does it rather than on the holy book itself. This attitude among Muslims gives some idea of the importance of this document in the Muslim mentality and the strength of its message, both yesterday and today. But it is the way it has been transmitted from generation to generation and the place it occupies in the early childhood years of believers—the tight interweaving of its music with training in reading, writing, and reciting—that gives an idea of its role as the source of our symbols and the cradle of our imagination.

A KORANIC EDUCATION

As a child I did not have the right to touch the holy book; only Lalla Faqiha (the lady teacher in the Koranic school) had that privilege. She taught me for my first three years of school by writing verses on a wooden tablet covered with clay. Every Friday morning each child received his or her prewritten tablet. We set to work to follow the tracings she had drawn on the slate with *smagh,* a special honey-colored ink. That was the way we learned to write. Friday was spent working at this task. Those who like me got *smagh* all over everything, especially the face, were gently mocked by Lalla Faqiha, who used to say that "the day you control the *smagh,* you will have learned writing, and perhaps neatness too, if Allah gives you his blessing." The tablets were carefully arranged against the wall at the end of the day, with the writing facing the wall. On Saturday morning they were all dry and the writing splendidly neat, and we felt great pride, because it was easy to forget that there had been smears at the beginning.

We, the smallest ones, were always seated at the front, in order to be better watched and to receive "special attention," as when a child fell asleep and needed to lie down, or when another shyly whispered "Washroom." As the children got older, they were allowed to sit farther back from Lalla Faqiha. Of course, when you are very little, all the whispering and interesting noise was behind you. But you felt safe. On Saturday morning all the children, holding their tablets, would sit down in their places on their own mats or cushions, with legs crossed in front of them. Under the direction of Lalla Faqiha, we began to repeat the mysterious signs that we had traced the day before. We repeated the musical words while trying to watch the line she was pointing to on the nearest tablet. Afterward she forgot about us as she attended to the older pupils and gave orders to her daughters about preparing lunch for her family. We went home for lunch or brought it, depending on how far each of us lived from school.

Usually children went to the *faqiha* in their neighborhood, unless there had been a big dispute between her and a child's parents. One time Lalla Faquiha struck my cousin ʿAziz, who was very proud and created such a fuss at home that all the Mernissi children (there were ten of us) were transferred to a *faqiha* who lived some kilometers farther away. There we could walk around in the medina for some hours both before and after school. We repeated the reading from our tablets from Saturday to Wednesday, which was recitation day. On that day another person entered the scene: Ba-Faqih (Father Faqih), the husband of the *faqiha*. After taking away our tablets, he made us recite what we had written. The pupil who hadn't memorized the verses or who pronounced them incorrectly was scolded by Ba-Faqih: "A whole week for three verses and you still stumble! How are you going to get six thousand verses into your little head? God knows if there is anything in that little head."

Children who recited perfectly were showered with praise. They were chosen to take part in the recitations that were given on religious holidays or when an important personage visited the school. If a child learned quickly and had a beautiful voice he or she was considered a prodigy, and as a result was able to shine in other domains later. I had a good memory but too soft a voice, so I was excluded from the first row in the ritual assemblies during my whole childhood. Later in my classes and seminars I always tried to have students rotate in order to create fluidity and a feeling of hopefulness.

A child begins attending the Koranic school at the age of three. At around six years old, you have already learned writing, mastery of the use of *smagh,* and the importance of neatness, and above all you have developed a prodigious memory. At around five years old you receive the first gift that signifies that you are an important person; a beautiful little Koran with calligraphy and gilding. My father gave me mine one Friday, but he took it back twenty minutes later when a cousin came up to ask me to go out and play: "When you have finished playing, you can have it back. I am going to put it on the windowsill. Then you just have to stand on a stool to get it. You must never drop it on the floor and never touch it without washing your hands and face. If someone asks you to go play, you must mark the page where you are reading with this piece of silk, carefully close it, look for the stool, and put Allah's book back in its place."

Throughout the Muslim world generation after generation of the faithful impress on their children the importance of the *risala.* Often in North African or Arab conferences or seminars I can recognize those who went to a Koranic school. They remember telephone numbers without writing them down; they take few notes during the sessions and recall in detail, almost word for word, conversations one had with them years before.

The Koranic school I attended in the 1940s was very like the one my grandfather described to me and the one his grandfather had described to him. And they all strongly resemble descriptions of the schools in medieval texts. Today, of course, the institution has been modernized. The *faqih* has a blackboard and a class list for calling the roll; new materials have been introduced. Nevertheless, the method of teaching remains the same. The Koranic school is probably one of the cheapest to run because equipment is kept at a minimum, and a single teacher teaches children of all ages in the same classroom. Children are supervised the whole day, except for rare moments when the teacher slips away and an older student replaces him. This is probably one of the reasons it has endured and why it still represents the only chance for millions of parents of moderate means to ensure that their children get preschool training.

But the great change is that nowadays there is a complete separation of children of different classes. In my time the division was by neighborhood; rich and poor were in the same school. Today children of rich parents go to English-style kindergartens or French-style *maternelles,* where they learn to read and write by reading "Snow White" and *Alice in Wonderland* in foreign languages, and only a few hours are devoted to the Arabic language and religious education. The majority of poor children continue by the millions to start life in the Koranic schools because they are the only day-care centers available. In Morocco, for example, the number of day-care centers financed by the government is minimal compared with the demand in a country where the birthrate is one of the highest in the world (almost 3 percent annual growth). Placing a child in a private modern child-care facility costs at least $100 a month, and one has to take the child home for lunch at noon and return him or her at two-thirty in the afternoon. Imagine what that would cost an average family, which has more than one child, in a country where the legal minimum wage is less than $150 a month. A neighborhood Koranic school doesn't cost more than three dollars, and the maids, factory workers, and craft workers leave their children there very early in the morning and pick them up on the way home from work.

UNEQUAL ACCESS TO KNOWLEDGE

It is in the types of knowledge available in each institution that we find the inequalities that today divide the Arab world and create an intense animosity between classes. While the children of the rich are educated from the beginning in both modern and traditional knowledge, the children of the poor are excluded from early training in modern learning, especially mathematics and modern educational games. It is true that many of the *faqihs* and *faqihas,* aware of the need to modernize their methods and course content, ask children to buy mathematics books and certain games. But most of them are not equipped to teach these subjects. This means that those who go to the Koranic school until the age of seven (the age of compulsory public education) start off with a handicap that is difficult to overcome, especially in modern science and foreign languages, which are given priority in Western-style preschool facilities. This difference in the cultural universe of Muslim children, depending on their social class and parents' income, is probably responsible for the xenophobia and rejection of the West in those who were deprived early in life of access to modern education. Chances of finding employment are in turn closely dependent on mastery of modern knowledge.[13]

It is interesting to note that most of the petrodollars invested in safeguarding our *asala* (authenticity) are aimed at the propagation of traditional knowledge. The money spent on promoting cultural life in our émigré communities in Europe finances the creation of Koranic schools, while only joint access to both kinds of knowledge can guarantee full employment to young North Africans in a very competitive European labor market: "The Banque Islamique de Développement . . . has financed, among other projects, the very beautiful and costly cultural center in Evry in the southern suburbs of Paris, where 70,000 Muslims live; there you find separate prayer spaces for men and women (no mixing), a library, a Koranic school, and a magnificent mosque with minaret. The cost of the operation . . . two million dollars."[14] Oil money is not being invested to redress the inequalities of access to knowledge, but rather under the cloak of the sacred to cultivate *taʿa* (obedience to authority) and the docility and proverbial fatalism that are continually dinned into our ears.

Nevertheless, judging by the dynamism of the protest movements based on the sacred, one must conclude that, despite all these attempts to manipulate the Koran, there is somewhere a power that these verses communicate. It gives a very strong sense of self and of one's rights, however much they are flaunted, and the energy to get angry and to imagine the world otherwise. This is what makes it important to familiarize ourselves with the words, symbols, and primordial scenes, the axial concepts surcharged with emotion, fifteen centuries old, that the dissidents reawaken and reactivate. Among them are *haqq* (right, truth) and *batil* (error, injustice). It was to the cry of *haqq* and *batil* that Imam Khomeini stirred up the wave that chased the shah out of Iran in the late 1970s. That same *haqq* was invoked by the crowds, furious about the bombs on Baghdad, in the streets from Lahore to Nouakchott by way of Kuwait and Riyadh. But each person put in the cry for *haqq* his or her own anxieties and frustrations.

A Mutilated Modernity

In order to understand why the word *haqq* stirs up the crowds, we have to go very deep into our collective memory. We must turn the calendar back to the zero time and plunge into the *jahiliyya,* the pre-Islamic era. What was Mecca like before Islam? All voyages are, of course, an adventure; they are a foray into *al-gharib,* "the strange"; we know it and we prepare for it. But it is impossible to find anything more *gharib* than the *jahiliyya.* With its violence and anarchy, the pre-Islamic era seems to resemble the life that is so familiar to us today. We have a feeling of *déjà vu* so troubling that we no longer know, as in the ancestral myths, whether we are going forward or backward in time.

Is the *jahiliyya* behind us?

PART II

Sacred Concepts
and Profane Anxieties

6

Fear of Freedom of Thought

Unlike the names Judaism and Christianity, which refer to persons (Juda and Christ), the word *islam* refers to a relationship: submission. The Arabic linguistic root *istislam* means "to surrender"—to lay down weapons ending a state of war (*harb*). *Istislam* and *tasallum* (to receive) result in a truce halting hostilities; *salam* is one of the words for prisoner of war.[1] The identity of the partners in this truce becomes clear when one reads the historical accounts of the year 8 of the Hejira (A.D. 630), the year of *fath* (success), when the Prophet returned to Mecca as conqueror and Islam became the official religion of the Ka'ba, the religious center of pagan Arabia. The truce was between the Meccans and Allah, with the Meccans renouncing *shirk,* the freedom to think and choose their religion, which was incarnated by the 360 gods enthroned in the Ka'ba. In exchange Allah guaranteed peace in the city, where violence was a problem. The word *shirk* is the opposite of *islam;* it is its negative in the formula that creates order on earth and in heaven.

SHIRK: FREEDOM OF RELIGION AND VIOLENCE

The freedom of opinion and religion of which the Universal Declaration of Human Rights speaks reactivates for Muslims the idea of *shirk,* which etymologically means simply "to join together," and also "to participate." It has a negative connotation because it is used to describe the disorder and confusion predating the year 630,

the date of the conquest of Mecca, when the Prophet tumbled the
gods from their pedestals:

> The Prophet, may the prayer and peace of Allah be with him,
> entered Mecca as conqueror; the people converted to Islam,
> some willingly and some reluctantly. The Prophet, may the
> prayer and peace of Allah be with him, still on his mount,
> made the *tawaf* [ritual circuits] around the temple and around
> the Ka'ba, where 360 idols were displayed. And every time he
> passed by a *sanam* [idol], pointing his cane, he declaimed,
> "Truth [*al-haqq*] has come, and falsehood [*al-batil*] has van-
> ished," for it is the nature of falsehood to vanish. As this sen-
> tence was pronounced, each *sanam* slid from its pedestal and
> smashed to the ground. The most important *sanam* was Hobal.[2]

This passage from Ibn Sa'd is the key to decoding not just one but
several enigmas that modern Islam confronts. The first is fear of
personal freedom, from which comes the ban on the artistic reproduction of the human face. The second is the exclusion of women
from politics, which is tied to the triumph of the monotheistic One.
Among the 360 gods of the Ka'ba, the most powerful were goddesses. These goddesses did not have the face of *rahma,* the tenderness associated with the nurturing mother, for they wallowed in the
bloodbaths of the sacrifices they demanded—sacrifices all the more
cruel because useless. These goddesses did not succeed in bringing
about the maternal miracle that they were supposed to guarantee.
The feminine would be doubly stamped with the sign of invisibility.
Women would be veiled, first because they were identified with the
violence of the goddesses, and then in order to homogenize the
umma (community) and cleanse the city of everything that smacked
of the pre-Islamic disorder. We will return to that primordial scene,
when Islam's social contract was concluded: peace in exchange for
freedom, *rahma* in exchange for *shirk.*

Before 630 freedom of thought did exist, and gods swarmed in
the Arabian heavens and had their place in large numbers in the
temples, and also in each household. At the time that Judaism and
Christianity were comfortably established among their neighbors
in the Mediterranean area, the Arabs continued to reject monothe-

ism and became "famous for the worship of idols," we are told by Ibn al-Kalbi, the author of one of the rare and fascinating works on pre-Islamic religions:

> Every household in Mecca had its *sanam* [idol] which the Arabs worshiped at home. When one of them was going on a journey, the last thing he did before leaving home was to place his hands on the idol and stroke it in order to become imbued with its beneficent power. When he returned from his journey, the first thing he did on entering his house was to repeat the same ritual, to touch the idol in order to become imbued with it.[3]

Shirk is the most appropriate word for translating the word "freedom" in Article 18 of the Universal Declaration of Human Rights, which is posed as an ideal to be attained: "Everyone has the right to freedom of thought, conscience and religion; this right includes freedom to change his religion. . . . " This article is the very definition of the *jahiliyya,* the chaotic pagan world before Islam. What it proposes is regression to the zero time. The United Nations translators, charged with putting the charter into Arabic, reeled under the weight of the task, using four words to render "freedom to change his religion": *haqq hurriyat taghyir al-diyana,* instead of the more appropriate word, *shirk,* which is found in the Koran, from beginning to end, not less than 160 times.[4] It is in that brief Article 18 and the concept of *shirk* that the conflict between Islam and democracy lies as a philosophical debate, a fundamental debate that was blocked for fifteen centuries, supported by the power of the palaces. The question is simply this: Do we love Islam because the police impose it on us? Obviously not. We love it for all the beautiful things that the police can neither offer nor take away—particularly a superb concept like *rahma.*

RAHMA: TENDERNESS IN THE HOMOGENEOUS CITY

In 1979 I interviewed a Black Muslim in Berkeley in order to find out how a Californian like him had come to Islam, and it was the word *rahma* that was decisive for his conversion: "That was the word. That was the code. I searched for it for so long. And here it was!" A Syrian friend brought him to the San Francisco mosque one Friday. That day the imam chose as the text for his sermon the verse that we are taught as youngsters and say when we have fear of the dark: "*Kataba rabbukum ʿala nafsihi al-rahma*" ("Your Lord hath prescribed for Himself mercy," sura 6, v. 54). *Rahma* is a rich concept with multiple facets: sensitiveness (*al-riqa*), tenderness (*al-taʿattuf*), and also forgiveness (*al-maghfira*). It is everything that is sweet and tender, nourishing and safe, like a womb. *Rahma* has its roots in the uterus, *rahm*. Rain is *rahma,* because it brings prosperity (*al-khayr*).[6] The *umma,* the mythic Muslim community, is overflowing with *rahma,* as is the relationship of love that links the members of a family and makes each one concerned about the fate of the others.

The clamor of the fundamentalist youth of today is, among other things, an appeal to that Islam of *rahma,* where the wealthy of the cities are sensitive to the anguish of the poor. Their outcry is the plaint of the unloved child of the family cut off from modern knowledge and its sciences that promise work and dignity. Reducing the outcry of the young to a declaration of war against the wealthy of the planet—that is, against the West—is to make a serious error in understanding their anguish. Peace in the world, and especially the strategies for realizing peace, depend in part on analyzing that anguish. If the camera is focused on the violence of the fundamentalist, the strategy is to cut him down. If, however, the focus is on his anguish, his fear of being forgotten in the great feast of knowledge, which is one of the most attractive promises of modernity, then letting him participate in the feast is the solution. This is what makes it interesting for us to go back to the Kaʿba in year 8, when Islam was only a hope for peace, in order to understand its message and what it had to struggle against.

Islam, with its sole God, triumphed in 630 because it succeeded in realizing what the 360 gods enthroned in the Kaʿba, expressing pluralism and freedom of thought and belief, were powerless to guarantee: the establishment of *rahma.* Violence was so widespread in Mecca at that time that even the gods were battered when they didn't please men. Muhammad's victory was swift and decisive because the Arabs suffered from insecurity, from *fitna,* violence in the city. The *jahiliyya,* Tabari tells us, was the gross behavior, the cruelty that resulted from ignorance.[7] An informed person cannot be violent and cruel. Islam proposed to put an end to that, to establish *rahma.* The first word of the Koran revealed to the Prophet was an order to read: "*Iqra.*"

HAWA (DESIRE) SACRIFICED

Like the other monotheistic religions, Islam promises peace at the price of sacrifice—the sacrifice of desire, *hawa. Rahma,* peace in the community, can exist only if the individual renounces his *ahwa* (plural of *hawa*), which are considered the source of dissension and war. The *jahiliyya* saw the unbridled reign of *hawa,* desire and individual egotism. Islam was to realize the contrary: *rahma* in the community at the price of the sacrifice of *ahwa,* individual desires and passions. *Rahma* in exchange for freedom is the social contract that the new religion proposed to the citizens of Mecca. Renouncing freedom of thought and subordinating oneself to the group is the pact that will lead to peace; *salam* will be instituted if the individual agrees to sacrifice his individualism. *Hawa* means both "desire" and "passion," but it can also signify "personal opinion." It is the unbridled individual interest of a person who forgets the existence of others in thinking only of his own advantage. Desire, which is individual by definition, is the opposite of *rahma,* which is an intense sensitivity for the other, for all the others, for the group.

From the beginning Islam was able to establish only a fragile peace, one that was constantly threatened from within by desire, the most unpredictable expression of individualism. Submission to the group was confused with *'aql* (reason), and all indulgence of preferences and individual desires was labeled irrational.[8] *Hawa* was thus equated with mindless passion. The threat of pre-Islamic disorder would always hang heavy over the city, for the danger is inherent in human nature. In every person sleeps a potential *jahili;* peace is only a shaky equilibrium. The words *hawa* and its plural *ahwa* occur some thirty times in the Koran as the negative pole of the ideal city. *Hawa* is the chink, the crack through which dissension and disorder can infiltrate.[9]

But—and this is the genius of Islam—*hawa* is not to be excluded or eradicated; it must rather be managed in such a fashion that it will not exceed the *hudud,* the sacred limits. Islam doesn't reject anything; it manages all things. Its ideal schema is equilibrium. In normal times everything can move within a state of equilibrium which does not put the security of the group in danger. Individual excesses can be contained. There is no clergy to monitor and punish, for the fundamental design is not a prison, but equilibrium. The key adage that mothers and teachers hammer into the little brains of Muslim children every day is *"aʿmal wa qayyis"* ("everything in moderation"). It is up to the individual, in the absence of a watchful clergy, to maintain a sense of moderation and never lose sight of the interests of the community. Individuals should enjoy themselves, but also keep a feeling for the collectivity. Human beings do not live alone in a desert; they should not shock the people around them. They ought not to deprive themselves, but they shouldn't exaggerate either. These guidelines keep *hawa* in check, for when the community is threatened, it can drag the ship down into chaos.

This is a possible reading of the Salman Rushdie affair: the imam, who watches over the cosmic equilibrium to see that the vessel of Islam continues to sail on a hostile planet, condemned the outpourings of the imagination as a deadly attack. Salman Rushdie is a writer of fiction. He creates from the imagination, the most indomitable refuge of individuality, a person's little secret garden that escapes all censorship, all compromise. An individual can be forced to submit, but his imagination can never be controlled.

It is also a possible reading of the cabal against the progressive intellectuals who have tried to introduce the Western philosophy of the Enlightenment since the Second World War. Finally, it is a reading of the declaration of war against the Muʿtazila, who in the Middle Ages proposed to discuss *raʾy* (personal opinion) and the place of *ʿaql* (reason). I could extend the list. The fact is that for fifteen centuries the imagination has been condemned to pursue its course beyond the *hudud,* outside the walls. That presents no danger if our great minds are in Paris or London or the United States. The imagination is the locus of all subversions; when the enemy satellites are keeping watch, it is not the moment to wallow in one's individuality. We shall come back to this issue, for the way in which the role of *ra'y* is settled is crucial for the future of Islam and its survival in the twenty-first century. It is absolutely necessary that the *umma* root its security somewhere else than in the ban on free thought. We cannot continue to stifle the imagination, the freedom to ponder and dream, for that is the locus of invention, the source of wealth in the electronic age! This is the great issue that Muslims are called on to confront and resolve. Fanatical, uncultured leaders, little versed in modern science, cannot give us a solution. They must drape themselves in their *rahma* and humbly reflect and learn.

Islam is essentially a dynamic, a fragile equilibrium between two poles: a negative (*hawa*) and a positive (*rahma*). It is a precise relationship between desire and power which keeps the city running and promises not only peace but also the family tenderness that delights us on some holiday evenings. That idea was very strong in Islam at the beginning and is still present in the minds of those who are the victims of selfishness and are reduced to powerlessness by insensitivity to their fate. If we don't keep this social contract in mind, we cannot understand why all the words that have to do with freedom of thought, creation, and improvisation are condemned and stamped with a prohibition, and why the great criminal of the century, Salman Rushdie, is a writer of fiction who draws from his imagination, not a scientist who describes reality.

THE IMAGINATION: SEAT OF ALL THE PERVERSIONS

In Arabic the imagination—the thought process that poses itself as detached from reality, as the withdrawal into oneself, the place of freedom that the group cannot keep watch on—is called *khayal,* which comes from the same root as the word for horse (*khayl*). The *Lisan al-ʿArab* reminds us that a horse is called *khayl* because there is defiance in its gait; it moves with arrogance. In Arabic we say

91

"yatliq al-inan" ("he gives rein to") about someone who acts in a completely egotistical and narcissistic manner.

The intellect is often compared to a horse, and of course Arabian horses are among the most beautiful and elegant in the world because they are fast. Horses and birds are powerful symbols in our vision of freedom. When I participate in an official conference in an Arab country, it often happens at the end that I am asked to sign some declaration or other. When I refuse, I am prey to the solicitations of those who tell me they love me and want me to understand where my interests lie. But their attempts to manipulate me stop as if by magic when I pronounce the fateful words *"Ana tir hurr"* ("I am a free bird"). The word *hurr* comes right out of the *jahiliyya,* where the freest man was the aristocrat, he who had no master, the opposite of *hurr* being "slave."

Al-hurriyya, "freedom," has always had an ambiguous status in Muslim civilization and has never acquired a patent of nobility or become a positive concept. Its meaning remains tied to the anarchy of the *jahiliyya.* F. Rosenthal is right to observe that "politically, the individual was not expected to exercise any free choice as to how he wished to be governed. At times, he did stress his right to be considered and treated as an equal by the men in power." Rosenthal also comments that *hurriyya* as conceived by the Sufis means submission to God.[10] However, the Sufis' freedom, abolishing the barrier between man and God, threatened the caliphs. In defining man, the Sufis gave him back his rights. The ban on giving the imagination and the mind free play is rooted in the fear of excessive individuality. The public freedoms (*hurriyat 'amma*) of which the Universal Declaration of Human Rights speaks have a strange sound in a society that fears individuality, seeing it as the source of all disequilibrium. If since independence the Arab states had put their energy into making us reflect about our liberation, as had been promised during the nationalist struggle, we would have been able to practice those public freedoms, and to compare them with our Islamic heritage. We would have had plenty of time to familiarize ourselves with the freedoms that frighten and disorient all those who hold an ounce of authority. Everyone gets hysterical the moment an adolescent or a woman announces the desire to be free. But let's go back to that *khayal,* that unfolding of the creative spirit, so still, yet capable of shaking armies and alarming every *shawush* and guardian.[11]

THE HORSE IS SMARTER THAN THE RIDER

I have always been enchanted by the sight of an Arabian horse, slim, high strung, quivering. So much energy within that shiny coat! So much rebellion chafing at the bit! I love to look at men and women who have this same quality despite all the risks it might entail, and the miracle is that I often find it when I search for it.

I have always admired even more the good Arab horsemen—that is, those who don't try to be smarter than the animal they apparently dominate. I am a dyed-in-the-wool city dweller, born in a place that dates back to the eighth century, where the streets are so narrow that the city gets its supplies from the backs of donkeys. Up to the age of twenty I played side by side with the very slow, more or less docile donkeys that moved slowly down the stone-paved streets.[12] On feast days, when I was taken to the outskirts of town to watch the peasants' games on their superbly harnessed and decorated horses, I always admired not the rider, but the beast. What enraptured me and the other children was that the horse was unpredictable. The moments we loved best were when the rider was thrown. In thinking back on those spectacles of my childhood, I realize that everyone, or at least the children, identified with the horse, not the rider. It wasn't until I was forty years old that I came across the Arabic proverb well known to all except me: *"Al-khayl aʿlam min fursaniha"* ("Horses are smarter than their riders").

What is certain is that the Arabs know better than anyone that it is ridiculous to try to master a racehorse, and by extension, to control the extraordinary freedom of the human mind. Just look at the way they set about educating us, and the defiance on one side and violence on the other that characterize the pupil-teacher relationship. One might say, without being too far off, that the basic idea is that a mind is refractory by nature, that it is stubbornly sovereign and resists all influence. If not, why should Lalla Faqiha have kept such close watch on me and beaten me with such vindictiveness? She knew that her power was only utopian.

Arrogance is condemned in the Koran: "Allah loveth not such as are proud and boastful!" (sura 4, v. 36). *Khayal* (the imagination) and *ikhtiyal* (arrogance) come from the same linguistic root. Imagining is full of risks for society because it is the power to create and to think in images—that is, to create a different reality. "To imagine something," says the *Lisan al-ʿArab,* "is to create an image of it." Creating an image is what was slapped with a ban, because the images that the pre-Islamic Arabs created were those of idols. They were the reproduction of their personal gods, or the gods of their tribes, each of which might contain only a few families. The member of a tribe was not so submissive to his tribal god as one might think, for if it thwarted him, he simply discarded it.

THE BAN ON IMAGES

In Arabic the word for image is *al-sura.* And today the only word we have for photographer is *musawwir.* Everyone has noticed the irritation shown by police and guards at official buildings in Muslim countries when you walk around with a camera. But it's not about the ban on photographing which exists everywhere in the world in museums that I want to speak. I want to talk about the exaggerated aggressiveness you encounter when you walk around with a camera in an Arab medina. I don't know how photographers make a living in Arab countries, but every time I have tried to take a picture of a tree or a door or a fly, the incident has turned out badly.

In 1987 a young Egyptian was determined to forbid me to photograph the Sphinx. I managed to calm him down by handing him my camera, just as one would do to mollify an angry child. But I was humiliated and fed up; he was spoiling my vacation. I asked in a small voice how I had disturbed *al-kawn* (the cosmos). Then, weeping, I told him that he was oppressing me and that I was weak (which is the best way to disarm an Arab man). My tormentor gave me back my camera, murmuring with embarrassment, "I don't know." However, he should have known that "the people who will be the most chastised by Allah on the Day of Judgment will be the *musawwirun*," as the ninth-century compiler al-Bukhari tells us in his *Sahih* (collection of authentic Hadith, traditions about the Prophet).[13] The angels, it is said, will not enter a house where there is a dog or a *tasawwir*—any representation of a natural object. This was how the cult of idols began; human beings fashioned images that they then began to worship.

According to legend it was a distant ancestor of the Arabs, Luhayy, who "first introduced the worship of idols into the Ka'ba." He is alleged to have visited Syria, and on seeing the people worship objects to have asked, "What are those?" They answered that they used them to beg for rain from the sky and to triumph over their enemies. He asked them to give him some, then returned to Mecca and placed them around the Ka'ba.[14] The ban on producing images of human beings forever links in the Muslim unconscious two things that have emerged as supreme in the modern information age: the image and individualism. Creation, imagination, individuality—so many facets of a fabulous, dangerous energy—are like mirrors and dreams. *Khayal,* Ibn Manzur tells us in the *Lisan al-'Arab,* is "the images that seem to exist, whether one is awake or dreaming . . . and that is the reason the shadow in the mirror is called *khayal* as well as what our body projects against the sun." The words that mean "to create," like *khalaqa* and *bid'a,* are dangerous and stamped with bans. All innovation is a contravention of the order of things. In fact, Ibn Manzur tells us, *khalaqa,* in the case of a human being, is synonymous with the word that means "to lie," *kadhaba.*[15]

Three words that are still brandished at us like weapons by the defenders of the faith are *kafir, mulhid,* and *zindiq,* which all mean the same thing: deviation from the right way. Religious fanaticism, like any totalitarian system, has its violent side. Its words function like a guillotine. If he who speaks in the name of God accuses a person of being a *mulhid* (atheist) or a *kafir* (infidel), that is enough to make the accused the legitimate target of punishment. Since creation and innovation mean divergence from the group, every word must be carefully weighed.

It is distressing to state that *kufr* (unbelief) is almost the reverse of *fikr* (thought). They both use the same root consonants, which are rearranged as in a dream or a slip of the tongue. The *kafir* is one who effaces, covers up the benefits he has received; he is, the *Lisan al-ʿArab* tells us, an ingrate who does not acknowledge God's having shown him the right way. The word *zindiq,* borrowed from Persian, means a person who doesn't believe in the Beyond and the Oneness of God. He is one who "makes things too limited for himself, for he deprives himself of eternity."[16] In a mirror effect, the three words reflect each other in the black hole of Satanism. *Zindiq,* synonym of *mulhid* and *kafir,* means falling under the influence of Satan, Shaytan, who plays his games, as we know, on the terrain of *hawa,* "desire" or "passion." Everything that feels itself to be cramped and confined when within the *hudud* that protect the city is Satanic.

Imam Ibn Kathir, in his commentary on the ritual formula that we pronounce ten times a day (at least), "*Aʿudhu billahi min al-shaytan*" ("May God protect me against Satan"), discusses one of the definitions of *shaytan:* "In the Arabic language *shaytan* comes from the root *shatana,* which means straying from usual human behavior and becoming conspicuous by stepping out of the ranks in some way or other." This definition of *shaytan* is important because it reminds us of the essence of order and the terms of the social contract and the meaning of rebellion: "*Shaytan* is the rebel, whether among human beings or jinn or animals. Everything that rebels is *shaytan. . . .* Shaytan has been so named because he is subversive [*mutamarrid*], because in his behavior and acts he abandons the behavior common to all, the behavior that leads to righteousness."[17]

The relationship between the general welfare and individual thought, the problem of the public interest and the flowering of the individual must be the focus for the reflection and global debate that Muslims are called on to undertake. This was the choice that was posed in Mecca in year 8: the public interest (peace) or individual interest (*ahwa*). But if the same choice faces us today, the answer does not have the same parameters or the same dynamics and does not call for the same solutions. The conditions for economic and cultural development are such that we no longer need to mutilate ourselves in any way. If the Arab parliaments began to function and the people democratically discussed the highways to be built, the schools to be erected, the jobs to be created, we would have a different vision of freedom of thought than our unfortunate ancestors of the *jahiliyya* had.

THE SOCIAL CONTRACT IN ISLAM: THE QURAYSH PACT

The idea of one sole God, which was the message of the Prophet Muhammad—a Meccan by birth and a member of the Quraysh tribe, one of the most powerful in Arabia and thus high ranking within a polytheistic city—was received as simply bizarre. The Koran is the best source on this inability of the Prophet's contemporaries to understand the homogenization of thought he wanted to bring about: "Maketh he the gods One God? Lo! that is an astounding thing" (sura 38, v. 6). It was not that the notables of the Quraysh disagreed with him; it was that at the beginning they simply didn't understand what he was talking about: "Does Muhammad want to reduce all the divinities to one? Does he want to hear us all say the same prayer? He knows perfectly well that each of us worships his own god."[18] Reducing all beliefs to one had something of the magical about it for them; in verse 4 of the same sura the Prophet is referred to as a wizard.

For the Arabs of 630, curtailing freedom of thought amounted to destroying not only the 360 gods of Mecca but also the thousands if not millions of little gods created every day by men in their homes and during desert journeys. One could speak of a veritable industry in idols, with each tribe, city, or group ordering a statue of its idol in accordance with its wealth: "If the idol was made in the form of a human being in wood or silver, it was called *sanam*. If, on the contrary, it was made of stone, it was called *watan*."[19]

Idols made of wood "would have to be the appanage of the nobles and the wealthy, as they were all imported."[20] The official idol, which would be placed in the temple or some other public space, represented an ostentatious investment of the group, in contrast to the small models produced by artisans for domestic worship. How were these cults to be consolidated so long as freedom of thought was the very basis of domestic life? But to treat

Muhammad's proposition to reduce the many to One as magic is to ignore the fact that for a prophet nothing is impossible.

Islam came into the world to bring into being the impossible. That is one of its central ideas and one of the reasons for its world-wide success. Worldly problems are not insoluble; their resolution lies in the ability of the members of the group to agree and be unified. This gives Islam its pragmatic character and makes it difficult to disengage it from politics. It does not encourage religious authorities to sink into meditation, as do the Hindu fakirs. Even persons in search of spirituality, like the Sufis, must keep one foot firmly planted in reality if they court credibility and if their main objective is to solve the problems of the city, even if those problems are extremely complicated.

In seventeen years, from 613, the year he began to preach publicly, to 630, the year of his conquest of Mecca, by insisting on this idea the Prophet succeeded in destroying the statues of the gods and goddesses and in unifying the Arabs around *al-wahid,* "the One." This was an astounding feat, if not a miracle, because at the beginning no one was convinced that peace required this great purgation of the Ka'ba. In fact, no one saw the link between pluralism and violence. For the Quraysh council it seemed simpler for the Prophet to bring his God to the Ka'ba and let others do what they wanted. At a historic meeting at the home of Abu Talib, the uncle and protector of the Prophet and the only man able to advise him, the Quraysh delegation proposed that "he stop insulting our gods" and "we will leave him with his God." After hearing the statement of the delegation, Abu Talib, who was himself one of the wise men of the city, turned to the Prophet and told him in all simplicity: "Son of my brother, this delegation is the most representative of the tribe to which you belong. They are only asking for justice by demanding that you stop insulting their gods and that in exchange they will leave you to worship yours in peace."[21] The members of the delegation waited anxiously for the Prophet to speak; they wanted to find a compromise and bring peace back to the city. The Prophet's response was that all he wanted was for them to pronounce one sentence, and one only, and then he would leave them alone, for that sentence would allow them to subjugate all the Arabs and to master the *'ajam* (non-Arabs). Relieved, the members of the delegation eagerly responded: "But what is that sentence? We could pronounce ten if you want." They were anxious to be conciliatory. The Prophet told them that all they had to do was pronounce the *shahada,* the first act through which one becomes Muslim: "Say: '*La ilaha illa Allah*' ['There is no God but Allah']." They of course refused, saying, "Ask anything you want, but not that."

Then the Prophet spoke the words that we still use today when we want to say we have no intention of compromising: "Even if you succeed in capturing the sun and bringing it and placing it in the palm of my hand, I will never change my mind. You pronounce that sentence or nothing."[22] The fateful consequence was that the city was thereafter literally torn in two. The accepted Koranic word for expressing this difference of opinion in the city is *shiqaq,* a schism that splits both the community and heaven in two and in Islam lays a curse on the number two. That word, *shiqaq,* occurs at the beginning of sura 38, which describes the preliminary negotiations of the members of the Quraysh council with the Prophet. When they realized that Muhammad would accept no compromise concerning the One, the decision to expel him from the city became the only solution.

Opposition to the One would forever have a negative color, and the words that express it today—words like *hizb* (party) and *shi'a* (group with a different opinion), which are rooted in that epoch—have a sectarian character. They are all ascribable to the split (*shiqaq*), the irremediable rupture. The word *hizb,* which is used throughout the Arab world to designate a political party in the modern—that is, Western—sense, refers to *junud al-kuffar* (armies of the infidels), those "who were leagued against the Prophet and plotted against him"—in other words, the Quraysh, who were for freedom of thought and multiplicity of gods. The concept of *shi'a,* which means "those who see things differently," is condemned in the Koran as "those who split their religion and became sects" (*al-ladina farraqu dinahum wa kanu shi'an*).[23] *Shi'a* refers here to the Jewish and Christian "sects," for that is the way Islam regards *ahl al-kitab,* the "Peoples of the Book."

In the beginning everyone was on the right path, then some went astray, and original Islam was born from the sects that had

99

departed from the path, the Christians and the Jews. The Prophet Muhammad, the last Messenger of God, came to correct the division and bring everyone back to the right path—that of Islam. Challenging the consensus, both before and after the time of Muhammad, means deviating. Islam perceives itself—although the West often forgets this—as rooted in the Judeo-Christian tradition, which constitutes its spiritual patrimony, but condemns the Jews and Christians as sects that perverted the initial message. If this dissension had not arisen, the three branches of the Peoples of the Book, those who have had the privilege of divine revelation, would be brothers united.

The splitting of Islam into Sunni and Shi'a is the historical proof that divergence of opinion is seen as a weakening of the group, and that it is better to cast out the disputing group and let it pursue its own course if it is strong enough. Opposition is seen as traumatic, a frightening situation because it recalls the violence of Mecca before the triumph of the One. The possibility for Muslims, both rulers and ruled, to tackle this problem by discussing it and rehabilitating *'aql* and *ra'y*, which was proposed by the Mu'tazila and the philosophers, was violently rejected in the Middle Ages and deferred until the nineteenth century. The debate was brought up again by the nationalists when concepts of parliamentary democracy were introduced in the wake of the colonial armies. As we have seen, this second chance to debate the subject of dissension within the community was also rejected. The independent states presented a solid front on the need for unity and after World War II declared war on local oppositions, imprisoned their leaders, and censored their intellectuals. On the brink of the twenty-first century the Arab world now stands in economic disarray because the main cause of that disarray, its undemocratic management, can be analyzed only by using sacred concepts that are heavily loaded against the individual and a plurality of opinion.

The hegemony of the sacred as the language of modern politics is all the more mesmerizing since in Islamic history rallying around the One has always assured a brilliant success. We must remember that the Prophet didn't begin to preach publicly until 613, when he was over forty years old. It was at this time that the problems with the Quraysh council, in charge of order in the city, are supposed to have arisen. However, the notables of the city, who were responsible for its security, decided only in 622 to expel the Prophet, or rather to silence his message. The year 622 is the year the break between the Prophet and Meccan officialdom reached the point of no return. In order to survive, the Prophet decided to emigrate. He left for Medina, but not to stay there. In the Muslim collective memory, emigrating is not a definitive move; it is only one step on the way of return, a detour to bring one back to the point of departure—Mecca, where the Prophet would return as conquering hero to reduce multiplicity to the One.[24]

The Muslim calendar begins at this time, the year 622, when the break between polytheism and monotheism was decisive. The miracle achieved by the Prophet of Islam was to have succeeded in demonstrating in his lifetime that his model was effective. In 630 he occupied Mecca and entered its temple, the Ka'ba, the high holy place of all the Arabs, as conqueror. The unification of Arabia was almost complete when he died in 632. The spiral of success and triumph had been set in motion. In 632 the Roman armies suffered their first defeat in Syria. In 637 it was the Persian armies that were crushed in the battle of Qadisiyya, the battle constantly referred to by Radio Baghdad and the Iraqi press during the war with Iran and during the Gulf War. Jerusalem was taken in 638, Cyprus in 649, Persepolis in 649–50. In 655 the Muslim fleet attacked the Roman fleet southwest of the Anatolian coast, and its commander, the Byzantine emperor, was barely able to escape.

The struggle between *shirk* and Islam was not a battle for a city. It was a cosmic battle for the occupation of heaven and the appropriation of time. All troop movements, any penetration of a foreign army onto sacred soil would reawaken the memory of year 8, called the Year of Triumph, and set the depths of the Muslim unconscious to trembling, bringing to the surface forgotten instincts and archetypes and calling to mind the symbolic events that express them. This is exactly what happened with the deployment of American troops on the sacred territory of Islam, whose psychological center is still Mecca and its environs. Riyadh, the modern capital, does not have this symbolic importance.

101

The religious language used by the American president in the Gulf War, sprinkled with "God bless America"'s, created the gravest confusion by giving many the impression that the satellites themselves were the objects of spiritual machinations. It seemed to be a religious war, a global conspiracy to destroy Islam and win victory for another religion, the religion of arrogant, capitalist America, even though Mr. Bush from time to time used the word "freedom" alongside the word "God." It might be said that the American president terrorized the Muslims as much with his ritual formula "May God bless the United States of America" as he did with the bombs dropped on Baghdad. In the sadly famous State of the Union message of January 1991, President Bush concluded by saying: "Tonight, as our forces fight, they and their families are in our prayers. May God bless each and every one of them and the coalition forces on our side in the Gulf."

Wide-eyed, the people asked, "But what God is he talking about?" The alleyways of the medinas were all agog. America, which the Muslim world thought viscerally materialistic, was fighting for its God. The common people did not understand the tenor of that speech, trumpeted by the media throughout the world, in which the American president explained that the object of the war was to defend democracy and freedom: "The winds of change are with us now. The forces of freedom are united. We move toward the next century, more confident than ever that we have the will at home and abroad to do what must be done, the hard work of freedom." The people were doubly confused: "Is democracy a religion?" the concierge of my building asked me the next day.

The blending of religious phrases with constantly invoked notions of democracy and freedom in the statements of the American president, all interspersed with the continual bombing of the civilian population of Baghdad, did not help the Arab masses see this electronic war as a modern conflict. It was a religious war, and the democracy and "freedom" Mr. Bush cited reeked to them of the calculating, mercenary attacks of the pre-Islamic hordes of the seventh century and the later Christian crusades. In cartoons Mr. Bush frequently appears as a *taghiya*, a pharaonic despot. Because it recalled the brute force of the pharaohs against Moses and his followers, the noble objective of the West, the defense of democracy, was completely undercut. The Gulf War, carried out through the most technologically advanced means in human history, plunged the peoples terrorized by the power of destruction into a search for guideposts in the area that eludes understanding: myth and its language of ambiguity.

7

Fear of Individualism

Rationalistic, devastatingly pragmatic, and above all fiercely individualistic, the pre-Islamic Arabs of the *jahiliyya* resisted the monotheism that had won over their neighbors for several centuries, preferring a multiplicity of gods whom they did not hesitate to insult and bully if by chance their wishes were not fully complied with. Throwing stones at a god, insulting it, and knocking it down was routine behavior.

The misfortune suffered by the god Saʿd, venerated by the Banu Milkan, a subdivision of the Mudar tribe, speaks volumes. The idol had the shape of a large rock stretched out at Falat on the coast in the vicinity of Jidda. One of its worshippers came to seek its blessing on a large herd of camels, which constituted his wealth. As he performed the sacrifice to the idol, he witnessed a disaster he had never expected. On seeing the blood of the sacrifice offered to the god ritually poured on the rock, the herd reacted in terror and galloped off into the desert. The bedouin flew into a rage, picked up some stones, and threw them at the idol. "What blessing can you give if you frighten off my herd?" he exclaimed in exasperation. When he finally succeeded in rounding up the herd he recited the following poem, in which he told the god why his fidelity could no longer be counted on:

We came to Saʿd so that my herd and I could stay united.
And now Saʿd has brought on our separation.

And what is Saʿd really but just an isolated rock in a sterile desert?[1]

In another instance Ibn al-Kalbi describes the misadventure of an even more prestigious god, Dhu al-Khulsa, who was viciously punished by one of his worshipers, Imruʾu al-Qais, the famous poet of the *jahiliyya*. Before attacking the tribe of the Banu ʿAssad to avenge the murder of his father, Imruʾu al-Qais went to his favorite god to consult the god's oracle since the expedition would be dangerous and he needed his blessing. When the oracle didn't give him the response he wanted but rather advised him against taking revenge, Imruʾu al-Qais became so angry he didn't hesitate to insult the god: "Go bite your father's penis! If it was your father who had been killed, you wouldn't have consulted me!"[2]

These anecdotes give us an idea of the self-confident arrogance of the Arabs. The relationship between the human and the divine during the *jahiliyya* was the reverse of the ideal to be proposed by Islam: it was the gods who were hostage to the will and critical reasoning of men rather than the other way around. The individual was sovereign, criticizing the god and constantly evaluating him according to his own criteria. This sovereignty of the individual imbued with his own power, this arrogance that permitted men to judge the gods and so to pose as their equals, was the characteristic of the *taghiya*, a man such as a tribal chief, a king, or an aristocrat who held earthly power through the cult of personality and despotic ambition.

THE *TAGHIYA*: MOSES' PHARAOH

In the Koran, *taghiya* means "tyrant," a holder of power that knows no limits. The concept has various aspects, each as negative as the other. Sometimes it is a matter of overweening pride that impedes submission (sura 2, v. 14), sometimes the despotic megalomania of such as Pharaoh, who is mentioned by name (sura 20, v. 24, 43). The *taghiya* is the leader who is contemptuous toward everything, including the divine. According to such a *taghiya*, only fools, in the sense of the mentally deficient

105

(*al-sufaha*), submit to a god: "When it is said unto them: Believe as the people believe, they say: Shall we believe as the foolish believe?" (sura 2, v. 13).

This complete and irreducible sovereignty constituted the major obstacle to the propagation of Muslim philosophy among the Prophet's contemporaries. One of the prototypes of this arrogance that opposed the divine was the Egyptian pharaoh, whose disobedience to Moses is mentioned in several suras. Pharaoh, who considered himself a god, suffers a bitter defeat in the Koran, his story given as a lesson for those who lack humility.[3] *Taghiya* is a favorite word in the language of modern Islamic fundamentalists; it is the insult they most often throw at the heads of contemporary Muslim rulers.

President Bush often appears in Arab cartoons as Pharaoh. A headline in an issue of the Moroccan daily *Al-Itihad al-Ishtiraki* during February 1990 has Mr. Bush declaiming in mock pharaonic tones, I AM GEORGE BUSH, I AM YOUR SUPREME GOD. According to the Koranic version, Moses urged Pharaoh to believe in Allah and to stop considering himself a god, but Pharaoh responded by massing his troops and declaring to them: "I (Pharaoh) am your Lord the Highest (sura 79, v. 24). Allah naturally inflicted total defeat on him, from which he never recovered.

Never have Koranic memory and sacred symbolism demonstrated their power more than during the Gulf War. The whole vocabulary of the press, as well as popular slogans, was drawn from that source. Jingles like "With the Koran and the faith, we will defeat America" ("*bi al-qur'an wa al-imam, sanahzim al-mirikan.*") were common. The fact that in Arabic "Koran" rhymes with "American" made sloganeering easy. There were also many references to socialism and democracy, but the concepts of *mas'uliyya* (responsibility), *qarar* (decision making), and *taba'iyya* (dependence) didn't carry the same emotional punch. Although President Bush had the privilege of being compared to Pharaoh, the Arab heads of state, who didn't have like power, had to put up with much less flattering comparisons, such as *himar* (donkey), which rhymes with "dollar," and with being reduced to the level of shopkeepers: "*Fahd ya al-himar, bi't Makka bi dollar*" ("Fahd, you jackass, you have sold Mecca for dollars"); *"Mubarak ya dhalil biʿt Makka wa al-Nil"* ("Mubarak, you beggar, you have sold Mecca and the Nile").

If in the cartoon in *Al-Itihad al-Ishtiraki* the cartoonist has dressed Mr. Bush like a Saudi prince, it is to reinforce the desired association between the American president and the Saudi regime. Both of them, like the Koranic depiction of the *taghiya,* can be nothing but transient figures; only the power of God is eternal. This archetype of Pharaoh-*taghiya* is at the root of the inherent instability of the Muslim political system, whose leaders, from the caliphs of old to today's presidents of republics, are easily challenged—and often physically attacked, in the tradition of the Kharijite revolt.

The populace has always been mobilized around the Koranic concept of *taghiya.* As long as democracy does not penetrate the popular centers of mass culture, the mosques and suqs—which might be achieved through education and participation in daily decision making—this orientation will not change. The modern Muslim regimes, which have plumbed the depths of sacred symbolism for everything that reinforces the bond of submission, have succeeded in subduing the masses for the short run. But for the long run it is the resentment of the oppressive power of the *taghiya* which Arab leaders have helped awaken, though their television propaganda carefully avoids any allusion to the concept of the despot. Islam is based on establishing an equilibrium between a positive pole (the ideas of *taʿa,* "obedience"; *salam,* "peace"; submission) and a negative one (those of the *taghiya* and *fitna,* "disorder"). Even if broadcasters on television talk only about the former, always present in the mind of the Muslim listener is the missing pole: the shadow of the tyrant.

Several centuries after the advent of Islam many Muslim leaders kept up the unfortunate habit of acting like Pharaoh, sometimes announcing that they were prophets (although Allah had declared Muhammad to be the last to have that privilege), sometimes taking the great leap into the void and claiming to be God in person. Giving in to this temptation generally cost them their lives, but even so the temptation still exists today, and the cult of personality is rife in many modern capitals in the Middle East.

107

FALSE PROPHETS AND
FALSE GODS AFTER MUHAMMAD

It can be said that the arrogance of the *jahiliyya* never disappeared. Well after the advent of Islam, Arabs continued to claim to be prophets; some, like the Fatimid caliph al-Hakim bi ʿAmri Allah, who reigned in Cairo from 386 to 411 (A.D. 996–1020), even claimed divinity.[4] The false prophet Musaylima (d. 12/633), called *al-kadhdhab* (the Liar), appeared in Yemen during the lifetime of Muhammad himself. Many rebels and political challengers who revolted against the caliphs claimed to be prophets: for example, al-Mukhtar al-Thaqfi (d. 68/687), who rebelled against the Umayyads: "Rumor spread that he was a prophet and had received a revelation from heaven." He left to posterity some speeches in a rhythmically musical language in which he tried to reproduce the poetic effect of the Koran. Many of the leaders of the Qarmatis, an extremist Shiʿite sect that committed such horrifying atrocities and terrorist acts that it was disavowed by official Shiʿism, claimed to be gods and prophets. Zakrawi al-Qarmati, who died in 293/906, claimed to be a god and required the people to prostrate themselves before him. One of his most notorious acts was his attack on a caravan of twenty thousand pilgrims traveling from Khorasan to Mecca, which he virtually wiped out.[5]

Stories about prophets who came to ask for audiences with various caliphs are legion. The historian al-Masʿudi described one of these surrealistic encounters with the Abbasid caliph al-Maʾmun, whose leaving his door open in order to learn what his subjects thought inspired many legends. The story is recounted by the caliph himself:

They led in a man who was passing himself off as a prophet.
"Who are you?" I asked him.
"Moses, son of Amran."
"Take care," I continued. "He threw down his staff and saw it writhing as if it had been a demon, and he thrust his burning hand into the bosom of his robe and it came forth white without hurt." And I continued to enumerate the proofs that were given to Moses to confirm his status as a

prophet. "So," I told him, "if you show me just one of the signs, one of the miracles that he performed, I will be the first to believe in your mission. Otherwise you will die."

"You are right," the man answered me. "I have only produced the signs of my mission when the pharaoh said to me: 'I am your supreme Lord.' If you will say that to me, I am ready to show you the miracles that I performed for him."[6]

The verse the false prophet asked to be quoted to him was none other than the one the headline writer put in the mouth of President Bush: "I am your Supreme God." A Muslim caliph, however powerful he was, had to avoid the arrogance of Pharaoh and show his humility before God, who is the only one to hold supremacy. Thus al-Ma'mun could not pronounce the sentence demanded by the false prophet, who was then able to leave the palace alive.

One of the most powerful messages of the Koran is the complete break between the divine and the human, and the equality of all human beings of all races before God; whatever their status in life, only their faith can make a difference between them. Supremacy, greatness, strength, sheer power belong only to God; any person who claims them is wrong. One of the ideas that divide Sunnis and Shi'ites is that the Sunnis do not believe in the infallibility of the imam, for infallibility belongs only to God: no human being, even an imam or caliph, can claim it. Making mistakes is the privilege of human beings and thus make it possible to criticize those in power. This basic equality between the strong and the weak, between governors and the governed, which is the essence of orthodox Islam, was surely one of the ideas that constituted a rupture with the *jahiliyya*. It introduced a new and revolutionary idea, unknown until then: the idea of *musawat*, "equality."

THE *UMMA* OF EQUALS

In Mecca of the *jahiliyya*, where trade connections provided the model of relationships, the safety of the gods was a chancy affair. Until the advent of Islam, blackmailing the gods (along the lines of

109

"give me some livestock if you want me to remain faithful to you") kept monotheism from establishing and proving itself.[7]

In this sense Islam is a long outcry against arrogant individualism. It was their boundless self-confidence that the Prophet demanded that the fiercely aristocratic Arabs give up by submitting their destiny to Allah. It was total, undivided submission that would permit the building of an egalitarian community. The annihilation of individuality before Allah, the Master of the Worlds, would allow construction of the other pillar of the Muslim order—equality. Along with peace, *salam,* it is the absolute equality of all, men and women, masters and slaves, Arabs and non-Arabs, which Islam guarantees, in exchange for the surrender of individualism. One of the most emblematic verses in this regard is verse 13 of sura 49, which the Prophet proclaimed in a speech in the Kaʿba once the idols had been swept out, and which is regularly recited at the opening ceremonies of intra-Islamic conferences: "O mankind! We have created you male and female, and have made you nations and tribes that ye may know one another."[8]

This verse condenses and articulates two messages: that of the *umma* formed of equals, and of the *umma* whose solidarity crosses borders and encompasses cultures, giving Muslims the beautiful sense of belonging, of universal communion, which is so striking when one travels abroad. From Dakar to Malaysia, the faces of merchants, at first indifferent, light up when during lengthy bargaining sessions an Arabic word escapes me. Then they ask me where I come from, and when I answer Morocco, they say, *"Ah! al-maghrib al-aqsa* [the Far West]. *La ilaha illa Allah!"* Suddenly I am given every consideration; a chair is offered, a cold Coca-Cola is brought from the neighboring shop, and the price of the bracelets of carved horn or of the glass beads I had taken such a fancy to falls precipitately.

It is impossible to explain the incredibly rapid expansion of Islam just by the fighting spirit of the fervently religious Arabs. That would leave out a very important factor: the insistence of the Koran on the equality of all, of whatever race or social origin. This tenet made Islam a peaceful, unobtrusive traveler, circulating in all simplicity, without armies or swords, using established trading routes. Islam traversed Asia and Africa, where social ranks often had the rigidity of castes, and it followed the great trade routes even to Indonesia and China, where one of the most threatened religions was Buddhism:

> Islam spread to points where Christianity had not reached. By the later Middle Period it was entrenched in East African islands like Zanzibar and the Comoros and at trading points all along the coast. Here it had no major urban religion as rival. But from Gujarat east, the urban societies were committed to Hindu and Hindu-Buddhist traditions. In all the ports of these lands Islam became important; by the fourteenth century it was even making headway (largely via south Indian commercial groups) along the Malay peninsula and the north Sumatra coast, where commerce passed between the Bay of Bengal and the South China Sea. Higher culture in the Far Southeast had always looked to the Indian mercantile groups for inspiration, and for centuries this had meant Hinduism; now it came more often to mean Islam, and with it the Perso-Arabic culture. By about 1500, Islam was a major force in all of the Malaysian archipelago and along the Indo-Chinese coasts.[9]

In 1987 I disembarked in Karachi for the first time, half asleep at four o'clock in the morning. What was my surprise to hear the customs agent, who gallantly offered to show me the city once day had broken, recite in a pure Arabic, when I rejected his offer: "O mankind! We have created you male and female, and have made you nations and tribes that ye may know one another." This same verse was quoted to me in mangled Arabic with a strong American accent by a jazz musician whom I went to hear in the Roxbury neighborhood of Boston. This was during the 1970s, when I was a student, and at that time many blacks were converting to Islam under the influence of Malcolm X. As a matter of fact, it was during my student days in America that I discovered how attractive Islam was for oppressed minorities, something that had never struck me at home in Morocco, where inequality and lack of solidarity are the normal state of affairs.

The popular sympathy Iraq enjoyed among Muslim countries during the Gulf War had nothing to do with the personality of Saddam Hussein, who was never the object of a cult of personality as Gamal ʿAbd al-Nasir had been. Saddam Hussein's war against Iran, in which thousands of Muslims were killed, left the masses in a state of confusion and disarray. The Arab masses are ripe for a leader; since President Nasir, who championed the idea of autonomy and sovereignty during the cold war before he began to imprison intellectuals, no one has succeeded in taking his place. The *Green Book* of President Qaddafi has been seriously read or commented on only by those who are guaranteed a job or an income if they do so. Other claimants to the role of leader of the Arab world have had the good sense not to be too persistent.

During the Gulf War it was not the personality of the leaders which carried weight in the decision to align on one side or the other. Rather, it was the *taghiya* schema that was operating, leading the masses to tilt to the side of Iraq. The emir of Kuwait and the king of Saudi Arabia, sitting on the oil wells that could change the power alignment if they were put at the service of the *umma,* both perfectly filled the role of the *taghiya,* for they were guided only by their individual self-interest. This is the way the Arab press and slogans depicted them: as pharaohs forgetful of the *rahma* that Muhammad's Mecca promised the world. President Bush, by insisting on making the whole world participate in the war effort, forced the Kuwaitis and Saudis to expose for the first time the amount of money they were paying to various Western countries. Learning how much the emir of Kuwait had been paying for French weapons was the opening shot in an inter-Arab democratic debate as, thanks to CNN, the financial details of the princely budgets were revealed and the flood of petrodollars invested in arms was duly exposed. The people became conscious for the first time of the cost of an airplane or a tank, and every time one burned up on the screen the young shoemakers, their hands working the delicate leather, mentally calculated the amount of money going up in smoke and compared it with their miserable daily pay: "'*Aqabt, ya farʿun*" ("Take that, Pharaoh!"). The medina was caught up by the full force of the sacred and by economic confusion that could only end in the condemnation of the tyrant.

112

Seen today as the culture most capable of channeling popular frustrations, Islam gives the faithful enormous expectations of social solidarity. The sacred, after long being utilized to pacify the masses and keep them quiet, is today taking its revenge on those who have manipulated it. It has become, as at the time of its birth, a force for the destabilization of privilege, whether regional or global. Harassed and hounded, the modern lay leftist movements coming out of socialism and Marxism have never been able to do the hard work that might have yielded up other schemas and other ideas. For many experiencing the collapse of democratic movements in the Muslim world, the cold war was the American struggle against the socialist Left. For them the CIA plot against Mossadeq was a representative example. The cold war derailed the cultural development of Muslim societies and, in Iran, allowed the imams to emerge as deformed mirrors of stifled aspirations: "What is happening today with the fundamentalists of all sorts not only does not renew the spirit of Islam, but is in fact a funeral cortege of petrified dreams that will disappear in the desert sands. Fundamentalism lowers intelligence to the level of emotional, visceral reflexes. And any drop in intelligence bears within it the germs of decay."[10]

Our mutilated modernity, void of the great democratic advances as well as cultural and scientific accomplishments, opens the way to the merchants of hope who are so familiar to us. Since we lack a vision anchored in the present and still less in the future, they are leading all of us toward the only area where phantasms can flourish—toward the past. They are unscrupulously manipulating its rich language, charged as it is with symbols and images saturated with emotion and bursting with hope, but connected to the subterranean vagaries of ancestral terrors. And well ensconced there we find the fear of women—a fear strongly linked to the disorder of the *jahiliyya,* which Arabs have never taken the pains to analyze coolly, as a first step toward moving beyond it. At the beginning Islam tried to break with the fears and superstitions of the heathen Arabs. But very quickly the example of the Prophet, who insisted on the necessity of change, disappeared from people's consciousness. The caliphs slid back toward the *jahiliyya,* locking women up and excluding them from the mosques. Women fell into ignorance and sank into silence.[11]

8

Fear of the Past

How can I dare to maintain that Arabs are afraid of the past, Arabs whose leaders daily trumpet that the past was the perfect time, the crucible of their identity, and that no present or future is imaginable without it? Our pre-Islamic past is called the *jahiliyya,* the "time of ignorance," and as a result is subjected to the *hijab* that also veils the feminine. But who knows better than the Arabs the haunting power of that which is veiled, of that which the *hijab* hides? The Arabs have dared to do two things no other great civilization has ever tried: to deny the past, a dark past, and to hide the feminine. And the past and the feminine are two poles for reflection on that source of all terrors: difference.

How can the new be distinguished from the old if the old is banned from sight, if the *jahiliyya* is a black hole, existential darkness?

And how, please tell me, can the masculine be distinguished if the feminine is banned from sight, if femaleness is a black hole, a silent gap, an absent face?

Can it be that the *jahiliyya,* that *hijab* of ignorance, is only an amulet against what is too difficult for us to accept, the raw, naked violence in the city that is linked in the inadequately buried past to a femaleness still more unbearable to contemplate—that of the goddesses who reigned in the Ka‘ba? For these Arab goddesses had nothing of the maternal about them. Their milieu was nothing but a pool of blood, and their sacred city a vast field of injustice and murder that neither the rituals nor the sacrifices succeeded in checking.

114

The *jahiliyya,* whose violence was miraculously suspended in time, has its revenge today by being reborn more monstrous than ever as Mecca is "defended" by American missiles—missiles sometimes fired by young women with angelic faces beneath their combat helmets. Are these young strangers, descended from the sky in war uniforms, parachuted into holy cities, aware that before them only goddesses handled arms and made blood demands in Arabia, where femaleness, like demons and dreams, has been driven into darkness?

These young American women have chosen military careers and perhaps see the Gulf War as an unhoped-for opportunity to liberate a country. But do they know that by treading Arab soil during this conflict they have awakened the giant shadows of those goddesses of death, pregnant with fifteen centuries of oblivion? Do the innocent blond heads peering out of the tops of tanks, whose function, death and sacrifice, is as archaic as that of divine weapons, know that they are unveiling a modernity that seems in danger of being mistaken for that spurned *jahiliyya?*

Ah, young American women, who exercise your democracy by dealing in combat helmets and death, let me tell you about one of the mysteries of that Arabia that for you was just an assignment, but for me is a tradition and a destiny. Let me tell you what my ancestors have put behind the *hijab.*

What is behind a *hijab,* the veil that means a barrier?

What is certain is that it does not veil "nothing." If there is nothing, there is no need for a *hijab.*

Normally only what is both powerful and dangerous is veiled. In our Arab civilization, the most famous *hijab* is that of certain caliphs. The *hijab al-khalifa* (caliph's veil), an institution of political Islam, with its protocol and rituals, was the subject of numerous treatises, the most entertaining of which are those of al-Jahiz.[1] The caliph was veiled because he represented a dangerous concentration of power—the power to kill. Can it be, then, that the notion of women in power is linked in our collective memory with violence and murder?

The answer must be sought in the zero time, the dark years of the *jahiliyya,* the years in which, despite the proliferation of gods, it was the goddesses who reigned over heaven and earth in Mecca.

115

And these goddesses lived on blood. Goddesses of war and death, they reflected in their blood rituals and terrifying demands the miserable existence of the Arab people, decimated by their own violence. It was to put an end to this violence, to end the *safk al-dima'* (bloodshed), that Allah sent his message to an Arab Prophet.

Sura 53, in verses 19 and 20, names three of the most important divinities in the Islamic heaven; then the subsequent verses utterly condemn them. They are al-ʿUzza, whose name means "power" in the military sense of the word; Manat, whose name comes from the same root as *maniyya* (death); and finally al-Lat, which is a contraction of *ilahat* (goddesses). Among the other gods mentioned in the Koran are Wadd, Suwʿa, Yaghuth, Yaʿuq, and Nasr (in sura 71, v. 23). But according to Arab and other sources, these gods were far from carrying as much weight as the female divinities.[2] First listen to the verses of sura 53 concerning these goddesses:

> 19. Have ye thought upon Al-Lat and Al-ʿUzza
> 20. And Manat, the third, the other? . . .
> 23. They are but names which ye have named, ye and your fathers, for which Allah hath revealed no warrant. They follow but a guess and that which (they) themselves desire. And now the guidance from their Lord hath come unto them.

These goddesses are identified by name because, among all the gods that filled the Kaʿba, they alone reigned uncontested in the two towns that were the cradle of Islam, Mecca and Medina.

THE CITIES OF THE GODDESSES

According to Ibn Hisham in his *Sira* (biography of the Prophet), al-Lat was the goddess of the Banu Taqif and reigned over their city, Taʾif. Manat was worshiped by the Aws and the Khazraj, the two tribes who invited the Prophet to Medina in 622 who constituted the majority of the population: "Manat . . . was their goddess and the goddess of all those who practiced their religion in Yathrib [the ancient name of Medina]; her temple was on the coast." Finally, according to Ibn Hisham, al-ʿUzza was the goddess of the Quraysh and so controlled their city, Mecca.[3] Ibn al-Kalbi gives us more details in his *Kitab al-asnam* (Book of Idols): "Manat was the most ancient; Arabs were named after her, children being given names like ʿAbd Manat [slave of Manat] and Zayd Manat. Her idol stood on the coast, facing the sea, alongside the mountain called al-Mushallal, situated at Qudayd between Mecca and Medina. The Aws and the Khazraj and all those who visited those two cities or their environs worshiped her, presenting offerings and sacrifices." The Aws and the Khazraj "carried out with the other Arabs all the ritual stages of the *hajj* [pilgrimage] except that they did not shave their heads." They concluded their ritual at Manat's shrine by shaving their heads there, at the feet of that idol, and it was "only then that they considered their *hajj* complete."[4] One of Manat's forms was a rock (*sakhra*); her name, stemming from far back in the ancient Semitic languages, in the beginning meant "count the days of your life." Later it came to be identified with destiny, which "gives each person his role," and ended with the meaning of *maniyya,* which is familiar to us toady as a word for death.[5]

Manat shares with the other two goddesses, al-Lat and al-ʿUzza, the very revealing title of *taghiya.*[6] This is a detail of some importance, for in the world of symbols everything is in the details. According to Arab sources, one of the sabers found in the temple of Manat had a new life under the banner of Islam. It was none other than the celebrated *dhu al-faqar,* the saber of ʿAli, the cousin and son-in-law of the Prophet, who would become the fourth caliph. After the destruction of the temple of Manat, "the Prophet offered ʿAli two sabers, and it is said that *dhu al-faqar* was one of them."[7]

Al-Lat, whose center was at Taʾif, Ibn al-Kalbi tells us, was more recent than Manat. "The Banu Taqif had built a construction around . . . a square rock. Quraysh and all the Arabs accorded her an enormous importance. . . . It was in her honor that the Arabs gave their children the name of Zayd al-Lat."[8] The military dimension of al-Lat has been well vouched for by recent scientific expeditions and research:

On the altar at Hebran, where we expected to find Dusares, he was found accompanied by a warrior goddess who had the attributes characteristic of Athena. This Athena was none other than the great Arab goddess, al-Lat, venerated from southern Arabia all the way to Palmyra, and the identification of her, which had been suspected for a long time, was confirmed for us by the recent discovery of an inscription.[9]

Armed and helmeted, she was recognized by archeologists on the altar at Hebran and the lintels of Souweida: "It was a warrior goddess, armed with a lance, being honored among soldiers; on the altar, receiving an offering from a veteran, she also appeared in armor and wearing a crested helmet." Although at the beginning al-Lat was the goddess of both war and fertility, only her military aspect remained prominent.[10]

AL-ʿUZZA: THE BLOODTHIRSTY GODDESS

But it is the goddess al-ʿUzza who represents most strongly the warrior dimension of the divine, linking the reign of the feminine in the collective memory with the age of darkness, when the insatiable deities bathed in the blood of innumerable victims, who were not always animals. Some link the enigmatic *waʾd al-banat,* burial of newborn girls, which was still being practiced at the time of the Prophet, to the human sacrifices demanded by certain gods. Al-ʿUzza would have been among them. Her name comes from the words ʿizz (power) and *quwwa* (physical force). She was worshiped in the form of a tree, and homage was paid to her in the Kaʿba, where she was represented by an idol, as well as outside it in a parallel rival temple dedicated exclusively to her. According to others she was supposed to be Venus and was worshiped in the form of a star. Let us begin with something tangible—her manifestations on earth, which were physically destroyed at the time of the conquest of Mecca in 630—before we consider her astral dimension, which seems to have survived, especially in the south in Yemen.

In his *Sira,* Ibn Hisham tells us that the Quraysh, the Prophet's tribe, whose influence radiated out from Mecca over the whole peninsula, worshiped al-ʿUzza at Nakhla, which was situated in a valley not far from Mecca on the route to Iraq. Some say she was represented by a tree, others say by three acacias. The fact that her temple contained a *ghabghab* (sacrificial altar) and an oracle, which was consulted by people from near and far, is evidence of her importance. She was "the most important idol of Quraysh; they made pilgrimages to her, presenting her with offerings to win her favor."[11] Her *ghabghab* was a *manhar*—literally, "place of slaughter": "It was a sacrificial altar placed beside a ditch or [dry] well into which ran the blood of the victims offered to the idol."[12] According to the Byzantine historian Procope de Césarée, the famous king of Hira al-Mundhir Ibn Maʿ al-Samaʾ (505–54) offered to al-ʿUzza four hundred human sacrifices, all Sassanid prisoners of war.[13]

Were the Arabs still offering human sacrifices to their deities in the time of the Prophet? Were these human sacrifices particularly linked to the cult of the goddesses, so that the reign of the feminine would be linked in our memory of the pre-Islamic period with the idea of violence orchestrated from on high? If that is so, is it not connected to the enigma of the *hijab* that hides the feminine and crushes its will at the risk of denying its existence? Does the negotiation of a new relationship between the sexes inevitably require a reconciliation with the *jahiliyya* part of our past and its reintegration into our field of knowledge? So many banned questions have long remained without answer, but they constitute the challenges that Arabs must confront if they are to construct the only identity that endures: that in which our whole human heritage is taken into account. But meanwhile, let us at least try to put into perspective the few clues we have.

WAS *AL-WAʾD* (BURIAL OF BABY GIRLS) HUMAN SACRIFICE?

Although some verses directly link *al-waʾd* to the demands of the deities, which would make it human sacrifice, many Muslim historians refuse to accept this thesis and advance other, less terrifying theories, such as that poverty or fear of dishonor caused parents to commit infanticide. Fathers sacrificed their daughters to spare them, in the first case, from dying of hunger; in the second, from falling into the hands of an enemy after a raid—the frequency of which, if this theory is correct, would suggest that such infanticide was a common practice. But the Koran explicitly recognizes in verse 138 of sura 6 that *al-wa'd* was inspired by the monstrous deities the people continued to associate with Allah, despite the clarity of his revelations: "Thus have their (so-called) partners (of Allah) made the killing of their children to seem fair unto many of the idolaters, that they may ruin them and make their faith obscure for them."

Tabari, one historian with a declared aversion to any idea of considering human sacrifice possible in the period of the rise of Islam, was inclined to believe that the poverty of families was the motivation for *al-wa'd*. But when he undertook an explanation of verse 138, he was obliged to admit the unthinkable: that it was the idols who demanded the murder of little girls.[14] In verse 41 of the same sura the killing of children is condemned as the result of ignorance, of the baneful influence of the deities who continued to mislead people and kept them from listening to the word of God: "They are losers who besottedly have slain their children without knowledge. . . . They indeed have gone astray and are not guided."

The idea of a deity who demanded the killing of children was inconceivable. To my mind, it is this phobia that explains the horror about the *jahiliyya* that up to the present day blocks scholarly research on that period. Before year 1 of the Hejira (A.D. 622), humanity had no history. There was nothing but darkness—only a zero. The fear that the *jahiliyya* inspires would explain all by itself why everything that recalls it stirs subterranean anxieties that we have never rid ourselves of.

The zero time is frightening in the same way that the future is— the future it so much resembles, with its violence that assails Arabs from all directions, from within and without, that swoops down from the sky in the form of bombs controlled by demonic enemy forces like the deities of the *jahiliyya,* each as mad as the other. Arabs never understood during the Gulf War, or even before, why the United States was so dead set against them. Why do the Palestinians, who are dying every day in the streets, chased and turned into fugitives, not mobilize the good will of the great powers of the world to stop that conflict? Whether the *jahiliyya* is behind us or before us is a question that recurs in the press. What have Arabs done to Allah which is so horrible that we are harrowed within and shamed, scorned, and bombarded without? The word *jahiliyya,* spread all over the media during the Gulf War, signified and condensed the problem that Islam came into the world to solve: the problem of violence.

In order to understand the connection between women and power which arouses so much hidden fear, we must establish the connection between these ancestral fears and the nonacceptance of the *jahiliyya.* The *jahiliyya* is the time that escapes our consciousness. The time that is not acknowledged is frightening because we risk finding there all our repressed images of violence.

We do know one thing: in the *wa'd* ritual it was the mother who buried the little girl alive, although the decision to do it fell to the father. According to Tabari,

> In the Rabi'a and Mudar tribes the man posed conditions to his wife: she could keep one living daughter, but she had to kill the second. When the one who was to be buried alive was born, the man left the scene, threatening to have nothing to do with her any longer if on his return the little daughter had not been buried. The woman dug a hole in the ground, then went in search of others who would come to help her. When the mother saw her husband come into view, she put the child in the hole and covered her with enough earth to completely bury her.[15]

In the lifetime of the Prophet, according to the Koran, only little girls were buried. We know, however, that one generation before that time the gods had demanded boys as well. The most famous case was that of the Prophet's father, who barely escaped being sacrificed. According to some sources, the Prophet's grandfather had vowed to the god Hobal that if he had ten living children in good health he would sacrifice the last to be born, who was Muhammad's father, 'Abdallah Ibn 'Abd al-Muttalib. The Quraysh tribal leaders dissuaded 'Abdallah's father from keeping his vow to sacrifice his tenth child, urging him instead to negotiate another solution with the god. Through the intermediary of the oracle, the god accepted the sacrifice of a hundred camels as ransom for ʿAbdallah.[16]

Some writers have questioned the credibility of this anecdote, saying that it is the product of the imagination of historians trying to make the very existence of the Prophet almost miraculous, since if his father had been sacrificed the Prophet would never have been born. Because Muhammad repudiated any association with miracles, these historians, checked in their desire to embellish his life with supernatural elements, did so underhandedly. Let's admit that the proponents of this theory are right: that the story about ʿAbdallah is a concoction of the historians. Their choice of a legend about sacrifice to the gods nevertheless remains significant. One doesn't choose just any lie, and one doesn't make up just any fantasy. Nothing is more programmed and coded than the sources from which we draw our lies and fantasies.

What is certain is that we know very little about the *jahiliyya,* which is so important in the construction of our identity. Exploring everything that has contributed to Islamic civilization, our whole past with all its historical and mythical component parts, with its "truths" and its "lies," its "high points" and its "low points," is necessary if we are to construct a dynamic, all-embracing identity. It is especially important to study what is hushed up, for it is there that we can recover the part of our unconscious heritage that kneads and molds our modern fears—fear, for example, of *al-waʾd* and the vengeful goddesses who demanded it. We must subject our past to study and analysis and mobilize our unemployed or self-exiled archeologists to teach us about the desires and whims of these deities, who didn't simply exist on earth but also occupied the stars. Venus (Zahra), whom we are so fond of that many little girls are named after her—Venus, whose radiance is so alluring in our Mediterranean nights—is none other than al-ʿUzza. At least we should be warned!

THE ARAB VENUS: KAWKABTA

If we go back to the religions of ancient Mesopotamia we find that the goddess al-ʿUzza was the Arabian counterpart of Venus, and both bore the name Kawkabta, which was of Syriac origin.[17] One of the most common words for star in Arabic today is *kawkab,* which is grammatically masculine; it is used several times in the Koran (e.g., sura 12; v. 4; sura 24, v. 35). Ibn Manzur, the author of the *Lisan al-ʿArab,* reveals to us that in his time (he was born in Cairo in 630/1232) *kawkab* was also called *kawkabatun;* "More than one [scholar] says that of all the stars, it is only *al-zahra* [Venus] that is called *kawkabatun*—that is, the feminine form is used while all the other stars take the masculine form, *kawkab.*"

Al-Masʿudi, a tenth-century scholar who is criticized by many "serious" Arab historians for being too anecdotal and for a tendency to get lost in details, seems to have been fascinated by the star cults and collected an enormous amount of information about them. He tried to situate the cults geographically and to identify their cultural environment, and especially to establish how they came to Arabia from Greece and particularly India. Yemen emerged as an extraordinary antenna, attracting and tapping all the world's knowledge. Al-Masʿudi described his visit in 336/947 to a temple dedicated to Venus, the temple of Ghumdan in Sanʿa, which was destroyed by ʿUthman Ibn Affan (who later became the third caliph): "Today . . . it is nothing but a mass of ruins that form a sizable mound. . . . It is said that when the kings of Yemen climbed to the top of that mound during the night, illuminated by torches, people could see them from a distance of three days' march."[18] Al-Masʿudi also places Venus among the Sabaeans in "the temples dedicated to intellectual matters and the stars," where she is represented by a triangle within a square—a very common motif in Muslim art which is found in the geometric tile designs that decorate the walls of caliphal palaces and mosques from Lahore to Marrakech:

There were also among the Sabaeans the temple of government, the temple of need, and the temple of the soul. These three edifices were in a circular form. The temple of Saturn [*zuhal*] was hexagonal; the temple of Jupiter [*al-mushtari*], a triangle; the temple of Mars [*al-marrikh*], a rectangle; the temple of the sun, a square; the temple of Mercury [*ʿatarid*], a triangle within a rectangle; the temple of Venus [*al-zahra*], a triangle within a square; the temple of the moon octagonal. For the Sabaeans these temples represented symbols and mysteries that they never divulged.[19]

It is time for us to unearth those mysteries, for our glorious modernity will depend on the reappropriation of all that is at work in the deep layers of our unconscious. Already archeological studies of ancient cults in Yemen have uncovered considerable data about the sacred in that region and particularly about the cult of Venus.[20]

Worship of the stars in pre-Islamic Arabia is mentioned in the Koran itself, notably in sura 6. The one who practiced it was none other than our ancestor Abraham, who lived in Mesopotamia and was saved by Allah:

> 76. Thus did We show Abraham the kingdom of the heavens and the earth that he might be of those possessing certainty;
> 77. When the night grew dark upon him he beheld a star. He said: This is my Lord. But when it set, he said: I love not things that set.
> 78. And when he saw the moon uprising, he exclaimed: This is my Lord. But when it set, he said: Unless my Lord guide me, I surely shall become one of the folk who are astray.
> 79. And when he saw the sun uprising, he cried: This is my Lord! This is greater! And when it set he exclaimed: O my people! Lo! I am free from all that ye associate (with Him).
> 80. Lo! I have turned my face toward Him Who created the heavens and the earth, as one by nature upright, and I am not one of the idolaters.

And so monotheism was established in Arabia for the first time, when the truth was revealed to Abraham, who renounced worship of the stars, particularly the sun and the moon. Later mankind forgot the truth that was revealed to Abraham, and Allah sent other prophets to remind the straying people: Isaac, Jacob, Noah, David, Solomon, Job, Joseph, Moses, and Aaron (sura 6, v. 85); Zachariah, John, Jesus, and Elias (v. 86); and Ishmael, Elisha, Jonah, and Lot (v. 87). Finally Allah honored the Arabs by revealing to Muhammad at the beginning of the seventh century an Arabic Koran (sura 41, v. 3), for the others had been revealed in other languages.

Although the other *ahl al-kitab* (Peoples of the Book), Jews and Christians, had practiced monotheism since the time of Abraham and renounced the worship of the stars, the Arabs had not taken the same step. Muhammad found them more fascinated than ever by the stars, and with no desire to forsake them. The Koran describes them as fervently committed to those cults. In verse 37 of sura 41, Allah commands: "Adore not the sun nor the moon; but adore Allah Who created them. . . . " In his commentary on this verse, Tabari tells us that Allah brings those who have strayed back to the right path by teaching that the course of the stars is regular only because they obey the divine will. They are the proof of the uniqueness and supremacy of Allah: "The sun and the moon must not be worshiped for themselves," he explains, "because they are incapable of self-guidance and of following their regular trajectory in the sky on their own. It is God himself who dictates their trajectory, and they are only signs of his power." In order to make us really understand the meaning of the verse, Tabari says elsewhere: "If Allah wanted to, he would be able to hide their light from you and to plunge you into darkness, unable to find your way, incapable of seeing what is going on."[21]

The Koran mentions worship of the sun as it was practiced in Yemen, at the southern end of the Arabian peninsula—where a woman, the famous Queen of Sheba (whose Arabic name is Balqis), reigned; "I found her and her people worshipping the sun instead of Allah" (sura 27, v. 24). Moreover, a sanctuary of the Banu Tamim which was devoted to worship of the deity al-Shams was destroyed and its idol smashed.[22] Even now the word *al-shams* (the sun) is feminine in our beautiful Arabic language. The Koran also speaks of the worship of another star, *al-shiʿra,* or Sirius (sura 53, v. 49). Commenting on this verse, Tabari says that *al-shiʿra* is a star that some Arabs of the *jahiliyya* worshiped.[23] Sirius, Jupiter, Mars, Venus—the celestial panoply displayed for our eyes every night—were also magisterial conquests by Islam, which was obliged to deploy its strategy not only on earth but also, especially, on the scale of the galaxies. The triumph of Islam ineluctably took place by pulling into its orbit everything that moves in the universe, with Venus in the lead.

Al-ʿUzza must be disinterred by our archeologists—al-ʿUzza, with her roots deeply buried in the earth, drenched in the blood of the *ghabghab.* We must recover that dark age if we wish to understand our archaic fears and to rationalize them. The pre-Islamic violence was so pervasive that many tribes no longer respected even the *haram* months, those in which it was forbidden to hunt and kill. Al-ʿUzza is forever linked in memory with disorder and killing in the city.[24] Like the modern era, the age of darkness was characterized by a cycle of poverty, violence, and disorder. Islam broke the cycle and taught the Arabs to appropriate the stars and time and to fabricate for themselves a present. But in order to do so, al-ʿUzza first had to be destroyed—not only physically, but also wiped out of memory: the feminine should never again be seen where power is exercised. The time of feminine power was to be the dead time, the zero time.

THE ZERO TIME: DEADLY FEMININITY

Al-ʿUzza was shorn of her power, but unlike al-Lat, she was hardly defended at all by her ancient worshipers. The destruction of her temple, just after the conquest of Mecca in 8/630, was a spectacular event. Khalid Ibn al-Walid, one of the most valiant of the great men, led the attack. The monotheistic order required that the feminine should be barred from the sphere of power, which coincided with the sacred. Woman would be the equal of man in all domains in Islam, since she was also a believer and endowed with reason and will; but she was henceforward to be invisible in the political sphere. In the palace of the caliph she had her place—behind the *hijab,* in the harem—the "forbidden space." Her space had to be separated from violence. Women must never have access to that which kills and introduces disorder: the power to govern the city, which was steeped in blood during the reign of al-ʿUzza, Manat, and al-Lat. Like the world, the caliphal palace was divided into two parts—a male space, where the sovereign manipulated power and used violence, and a female space, the harem, where women were distanced from everything that had any semblance of power.

Today the parliaments of the Arab states seem to take themselves for the caliphal palaces of yesteryear. There only men discuss and decide the fate of the world and its peoples while women wait at home, veiled and silent. The power of the feminine will henceforth be aligned with the *jahiliyya,* the zero time of Islam. The Arabs know very well that "zero" does not mean "nothing." It was they who had the genius to rehabilitate this number (which they are supposed to have taken from the Indians, who were already using it), which allowed humanity to make the prodigious intellectual leap that started it on the road to modern mathematics. Women were veiled not only because their invisibility made it possible to forget difference and create the fiction that the *umma* was unified because it was homogeneous, but above all in order to make people forget what the Arabs of the *jahiliyya* knew only too well: it is the body and its unconquerable sexuality that is the irreducible fortress of sovereign individuality. The Arabs of the *jahiliyya* could allow themselves to insult their gods, to be haughty and insolent, for they knew that they were irreparably mortal. They didn't believe in the existence of another world and found the idea of resurrection (*al-baʿth*) preached by the Prophet the sheerest fantasy.

Al-baʿth, resurrection after death, gives the Muslim immortality. It accomplishes two miracles with one stroke: it ties the life of the individual to the trajectory of the stars, and it effaces the uterus. A man born of the uterus of a woman is inevitably mortal. The Arabs of the *jahiliyya* did not recognize the law of paternity. To them it was a secondary consideration because they thought themselves mortal and couldn't imagine how God would make them born again from a heap of bones:

49. And they say: When we are bones and fragments, shall we, forsooth, be raised up as a new creation?
50. Say: Be ye stones or iron
51. Or some created thing that is yet greater in your thoughts! Then they will say: Who shall bring us back (to life). Say: He who created you at the first. Then will they

shake their heads at thee, and say: When will it be? Say: It will perhaps be soon; (sura 17)

Becoming immortal was something unimaginable for a pre-Islamic Arab, who distrusted everything and believed only what he could see: individuals are born of women, they die and become dust. Paternity has meaning only for a man who thinks himself immortal, who sees himself as part of a succession of generations, as integrated into a design that goes beyond the brief, fleeting individual experience. For the "ignorant" people of the *jahiliyya,* coming back to life after death was "mere magic" (sura 11, v. 7), and it was not easy for Islam to lead these rough bedouin to be on intimate terms with the stars and able to make use of them.[25]

The Arabs were to be resurrected in the Beyond; the Muslim would have the privilege of *ba'th.* He would be reborn, whereas invisibility was the law for women, who are the bearers of finitude, with the mark of stupid, foolish death in their wombs.

The reform movements of the last two centuries have more or less all presented themselves as a renaissance (*inbi'ath*). As the most recent example, the word *ba'th* is that used by the founders of Saddam Hussein's Ba'th party to express their faith in the rebirth of the Arab world in the modern age. Like the other monotheistic religions, Islam completely changed the relationship of the believer to time, enriching it and interweaving the believer's life with the movement of the stars.

Islam gave the faithful immortality in exchange for submission. The Arabs were to become immortal. A great Beyond opened to them the royal road to the conquest of time. They would no longer die; Paradise awaited them. Because the child born of the womb of the woman is mortal, however, the law of paternity was instituted to screen off the uterus and woman's will within the sexual domain. Islam offered the Arabs two gifts, the idea of paternity and the Muslim calendar—gifts that are the two faces of the same thing, the privilege of eternity. The new code of immortality was to be inscribed on the body of woman. Henceforth the children born of the uterus of a woman would belong to their father, and he is certain of gaining Paradise if he submits to the divine will.

The Arabs, then, entered history by the main gate: the mastery of time through the submission of the world to an Arab calendar. In their dealings with the Arabs, the Persians and Romans were obliged to use the Arab calendar of the Hejira—a calendar whose year 1 erased the previous 622 years of the Christian calendar and thousands of years of the Jewish one. Masters of time and masters of women, the Muslims, with Koran in one hand and calendar in the other, set forth on the conquest of the world, succeeding with lightning speed for some centuries. Today they compute their debt and its amortization by the Christian calendar. As for women, under the compulsory chador, armed with university degrees and the contraceptive pill they challenge and threaten the city.

9

Fear of the Present

In the eleventh century the powerful Fatimid caliph al-Hakim ordered the astronomer, optician, and mathematician Ibn al-Haytham to use his science to regulate the waters of the Nile. In an attempt to solve his political problems, the caliph commanded the astronomer to find a means of halting the Nile's disastrous fluctuations between flood and drought which brought on famine and inflation, resulting in riots and political instability. Ibn al-Haytham tackled the task but failed. His knowledge of mathematics proved inadequate to find a solution. Al-Hakim dismissed him from court, and Ibn al-Haytham finished out his days as a copyist. Nonetheless, his treatise on optics became a classic text and was used in the West in a Latin translation up to the time of Kepler.[1]

Today few Arab heads of state would dream of an ecological approach on this scale as a solution to the problems of unemployment and instability; their solution would more likely be to send an army into the streets or to imprison the rioters. Facing an ecological disaster, they would turn not to an Arab scientific team but rather to an American firm, just as the emir of Kuwait did to put the oil wells back in operation. It is not that there are not enough Arab brains to recruit; some thirty thousand university graduates in engineering from Muslim countries are now living in Europe and America, where many have become responsible for research and development in their professions.[2] One finds 754 such specialists listed in the latest edition of *American Men and Women of Science,* among whom are 225 physicists and mathematicians. But why, unlike the eleventh-century caliph, does neither the emir of Kuwait nor any other Arab head of state think of calling on that army of scientific Muslims and "commanding" from them research aimed at solving the problem of political instability and economic neglect?

Al-Hakim tied sovereignty to the Muslim calendar, which anchors political decision making to the movements of the stars and the mastery of time. Today Muslims are exiles in time, and their exile is symbolized by the shrinking of the field of activities that are regulated by our calendar. Everything important is controlled by Western time, from airline schedules to the payment of the foreign debt. For al-Hakim, the Muslim sovereign, time and the paths of the stars were momentous questions. Under his rule, Cairo became a meeting place for the world's great astronomers. As a Shi'ite Muslim, he knew better than anyone the importance of light and the intimate relationship with the stars which gave meaning to a life. The Fatimids gave their princely fabrics the color of light; their robes and turbans were white and gold. For them, astronomy was both an avocation and a vehicle of political decision making. Just as modern-day Muslims do in primary school, al-Hakim as a child recited verses 32 and 33 of sura 14:

32. Allah is He Who created the heavens and the earth, and causeth water to descend from the sky, thereby producing fruits as food for you, and maketh the ships to be of service unto you, that they may run upon the sea at His command, and hath made of service unto you the rivers;
33. And maketh the sun and the moon, constant in their courses, to be of service unto you, and hath made of service unto you the night and the day.

Al-Hakim was so fascinated by the cycle of the moon and the movement of the stars that he would spend whole nights observing them, forgetting to sleep, and finally forgetting the world. He ended up sinking into the madness that lies in wait for those who think too much about death. For what is our love of the stars if it is not fear of death? We depart, but they remain. This is the message of their mysterious, steady twinkling.[3] But that is another story.

131

What I want to talk about here is the story of how Arabs have been dispossessed of time. What was so psychologically traumatic about the Gulf War was that it revealed that the heavens and the stars were in the service of the United States. What is Islam if it does not put at the service of Muslims the stars and time, which are given meaning and importance through our calendar?

TARIKH: CALENDAR AND HISTORY

The idea that Islam is the mastery of time and the anchoring of human life to the course of the stars is found throughout the Koran. Verse 6 of sura 10 says:

> He it is who appointed the sun a splendour and the moon a light, and measured for her stages, that ye might know the number of the years, and the reckoning. Allah created not (all) that save in truth. He detaileth the revelations for people who have knowledge.

Being Muslim means being master of time and the stars, which Allah created to permit us to establish a *tarikh,* "calendar." Isn't it revealing that the word *tarikh* means both "calendar" and "history"? The *tarikh* is the calendar that allows us to situate ourselves in the present, to mark the dates for actions to be undertaken, but also wisely to align behind us the accumulation of the days and years gone by. A people without a *tarikh* have neither a present nor a history; they simply don't exist. There are of course many Arabic words that denote time: for example, *zaman, dahr, waqt.* But the idea of *tarikh* entwines time with human endeavor; it is in time that action unfolds and events follow on one another.

With the idea of *tarikh* we come upon the most secret, least conscious dimension of Islam, although certainly a crucial one: the temporal dimension, which produces anxiety about death. We fear death because we want more time to laugh and love. If today religion is enjoying a resurgence, it is because all existing science has not dealt in any real way with the unbearable brevity of our days.[4] The Muslim calendar, *tarikh,* which begins with year 1 of the

Hejira, resolves the fear of death with a single concept—*baʿth* (resurrection). This concept "fatefully" ties together the movement of the stars, the flux of day and night, and woman, life's starting point.

Is it possible that our idea of woman, who gives birth, thus beginning individual time, is in some way commingled in the deep obscurity of our unconscious with our apprehension of the end of life's span, of that death that religion has precisely come to deny and erase? Can it be that the phobia about the mixing of the sexes, about women's invasion of the streets and Muslim public places, has something to do with the needed reconsideration of our relationship to death—that is, to time? Can it be that the sexual crisis that is so well expressed by the obsession with the *hijab* is in fact a crisis about our perception of time? Can it be that woman, signifying birth and thus inevitably death, obliges Muslims to reconsider the present, the time they so scorn and neglect? The dream of immortality that the religion proposes pushes the fear of death from consciousness, but at the price of devaluing present time, the time marked by the rhythm of the stars in their courses and the regular appearance of the sun and moon, yesterday and today. We die a little at each sunset. In lands where sunset has a spectacular splendor, as on the Atlantic coast of Morocco, the anguish that overtakes us when the sun sinks into the sea is the realization that there is one day less between us and the end. Perhaps more than any other religion, Islam pays particular attention to the stars and the march of time.

Awareness of the stars and their light pervades the Koran, which reflects the brightness of the heavenly bodies in many verses. The blossoming of mathematics and astronomy was a natural consequence of this awareness. Understanding the cosmos and the movements of the stars means understanding the marvels created by Allah. There would be no persecuted Galileo in Islam, because Islam, unlike Christianity, did not force people to believe in a "fixed" heaven. In the Christian cosmos, Bertrand Russell tells us, "the orthodox theory was the Ptolemaic, according to which the earth is at rest in the centre of the universe, while the sun, moon, planets, and system of fixed stars revolve around it."[5] This world view is very different from that of Islam: in the Koran the whole universe moves. This meant that the theorizing of mathematicians and astronomers could not threaten religious authority, as it did in the Catholic church, which—fearing that if the earth revolved around the sun, ecclesiastical authority would collapse—found itself obliged to suppress the savants.

> While it was thought that the sun and moon, the planets and the fixed stars, revolved once a day about the earth, it was easy to suppose that they existed for our benefit, and that we were of special interest to the Creator. But when Copernicus and his successors persuaded the world that it was we who rotate while the stars take no notice of our earth; when it appeared further that our earth is small compared to several of the planets . . . it became increasingly difficult to believe that such a remote and parochial retreat could have the importance to be expected of the home of Man, if Man had the cosmic significance assigned to him in traditional theology. Mere considerations of scale suggested that perhaps we were not the purpose of the universe.[6]

Islam cannot be threatened by the discoveries of astronomy, such as the observation of new galaxies, because its vision is of a cosmos in movement. Threats to its authority do not come from outside, but from within human beings. It is imagination, and the irreducible sovereignty of the individual which engender disequilibrium and tension. A Galileo challenging the authority of Islam must be not a scientist but an essayist or novelist, a Salman Rushdie, and exploration of the psyche will surely be the arena of all future sedition.[7] It is certainly not the stars that pose a problem for Islam; in fact, it is their movement and their power that constitute, permeate, and inspire it. Shi'ite Islam would be incomprehensible if one ignored the role played by light and the stars.[8]

In the Islamic vision, the wealth of the earth and the heavens belongs to those who link earthly governance to the trajectory of the stars; everything else follows from that. Today our heads of state, who live without looking at the sky and have no passion for astronomy, the favorite pastime of the caliphs of old, are completely detached from any relationship to the stars and their movement. Intimate knowledge of the sky and the stars is the monopoly of the Christian West. Like idiots we continue to sing "*Ya layl, ya qamar*" ("O night, O moon"), the inevitable refrain of every love song, all the while ignoring the fact that both night and moon now belong to the masters of artificial satellites. The *tarikh* was one of the precious gifts that God gave to some miserable pre-Islamic Arabs who were being ignored and scorned in their time. We can see that scorn in the response of the king of Persia to a letter sent by the Prophet in year 6 of his own calendar:

> The Prophet sent eight ambassadors to eight princes, to call them to God. . . . The king of Persia, Kasra Parwiz, after reading the Prophet's letter, tore it up and threw it in the face of the envoy, saying: "How does that man, who is my subject, dare to address such a letter to me?" He then wrote a letter to Badsan, his governor in Yemen, saying: "That Arab who has suddenly appeared in the Hijaz has sent me an unacceptable letter. Send two reliable men to bring him before me in chains so that I can see how best to deal with him."[9]

If Islam and its Prophet make sense on the eve of the twenty-first century, it is because the *risala,* the message of the Koran, is nothing but a series of prescriptions about how to escape from the scorn of the international powers by appropriating time—that is, putting the faithful in orbit and attaching their lives to the dance of the stars. This poses the interesting questions of who the first to have the idea of the calendar was, and why the year 622 was chosen as its starting point.

CREATION OF THE MUSLIM CALENDAR

Who was the first to have the idea of the calendar? The answers to that question vary. According to one, it was the Prophet who proposed establishing the *tarikh* soon after his arrival in Medina (thus, right after the Hejira). Another version of the origin of the calendar says that it was during the time of caliph ʿUmar that its need was felt:

When the Prophet, may the prayer and peace of Allah be with him, arrived in Medina, and he arrived in the month of Rabi' the first, he gave the order to institute the *tarikh*. Some say that they began to use dates beginning with his arrival. But others say that the first who gave the order to institute the *tarikh* was 'Umar Ibn al-Khattab.[10]

Because the Prophet had a cosmic dimension to his thinking which none of his Companions had, to me it seems more likely that it was he who instituted the calendar on his arrival in the new city. It should not be forgotten that he also changed the direction of the *qibla,* that is, of prayer, shortly after his arrival in Medina. The Muslims had been praying in the direction of Jerusalem for several months, but once the Jewish community of Medina became hostile, the Prophet received the order from God to change the direction of the *qibla* to Mecca. One anecdote concerning 'Umar gives an idea of what it was like to live in a society in the throes of a revolutionary turnabout of attitudes:

Al-Sha'bi said that Abu Musa al-Ash'ari wrote to 'Umar: "I received some letters from you without a date." 'Umar assembled the people to consult with them. Some said that dating should begin with the moment when the Prophet first received the revelation. Others said that it would be better to date from the time of the Hejira of the Prophet. 'Umar finally opted for taking the Hejira as the start, for, he said, "it was at that moment that there was truly a break between *al-batil* [error] and *al-haqq* [truth]."[11]

'Umar, the second caliph, came to power thirteen years after the death of the Prophet; his official Abu Musa al-Ash'ari was one of the first Muslim governors sent abroad to administer conquered territories. The two moments suggested as symbolic of the break with the past and the beginning of a new time were thus the date that Allah revealed to the Prophet his mission and the time of the Hejira, thirteen years later. The Prophet was fifty-three years old when he decided to leave Mecca, which had become antagonistic and violent toward him since the city notables realized that he did not intend to compromise but rather to destroy the idols of the Ka'ba. If this second option is the true one, the beginning of the calendar coincided with the access of the Muslims to the management of the riches of the world.

In another version I find intriguing, 'Umar is supposed to have not even understood what dating meant:

> According to Ibn Sirin, a man stood up and demanded that 'Umar Ibn al-Khattab begin assigning dates. 'Umar is supposed to have asked: "What does assigning dates mean?" They answered him: "It is something that al-'ajam [non-Arabs] do; they write in such-and-such a month of such-and-such a year. 'Umar Ibn al-Khattab then said, "Very well." They then decided to begin using dates. Then the question arose of finding out when we were going to begin. Some said that the beginning should be the moment when the Prophet received the revelation; others said the date of his death; still others suggested the date of the Hejira as the beginning point.[12]

Here we hear the very idea of a calendar questioned in 'Umar's "What does assigning dates mean?" However, we must approach this account with caution; 'Umar was no savage bedouin, but a member of the merchant aristocracy of that city of cities, Mecca. And when you say merchant, you say documents dated and registered. The Arabs did not just excel at managing debt; Mecca was situated astride the great international trading route of the time. The Companions of the Prophet had trade in their blood. They amazed the Ansar because they always found time for making war for the triumph of Islam while also conducting business in their rare moments of repose. It is difficult to believe that 'Umar didn't know what assigning dates meant. It seems more plausible that in his time it was decided to use the calendar in a systematic and official fashion as a manifestation and incarnation of the new administration that would quickly become an empire.

There is one detail in the story that is very significant for the present state of confusion in the Muslim world. During the session related above, when 'Umar was contemplating the institution of the calendar, some of his entourage suggested using the Persian or Roman calendar:

> When 'Umar said, "Find something for the people to use to get their bearings," some said, "Why not write the dates in the Roman manner?" . . . Others said, "Why not borrow the Persians' calendar?" However, the majority of the people opted for the date of the Hejira as the beginning date, and they counted the number of years the Prophet had spent in Medina.[13]

Those who suggested borrowing the Persian or Roman calendar certainly had no understanding of Muhammad's new order, which was based on autonomy vis-à-vis the neighboring powers. This anecdote reminds us how dependent we have become, since we now find it "natural" to follow the Western calendar.

The pre-Islamic Arabs did not have a unified calendar. According to Tabari, "each tribe established its own *tarikh*, beginning with an event that took on a special significance for it, a disaster, a famine, a war. . . . "[14] With each tribe creating its *tarikh* as it pleased, one can imagine the resulting confusion in intertribal and intercity exchanges and communications. The Quraysh, the tribe of the Prophet which controlled Mecca, had a calendar that dated events beginning with the *'am al-fil* (Year of the Elephant), when the Abyssinian army, mounted on those impressive beasts, conquered Mecca around A.D. 570, the year of the Prophet's birth.[15] It was decided to begin the new calendar with this date because seeing elephants in the environs of Mecca, not a common occurrence, represented an unforgettable landmark event.

The lack of unity among the Arabs in the handling of time is well illustrated in the muddle created by that curious month Nasi'. According to Tabari, the Arabs named Nasi' the month for hunting or conducting raids, whereas custom had declared it *shahr haram*, the month when all violence was forbidden.[16] For al-Mas'udi, this month of Nasi' had another function: it was intercalated every three years to compensate for the short lunar months. He begins, as was his custom, by situating us within the context of the time before telling us precisely what Nasiʾ is:

> The lunar months begin with Muharram and count 354 days, being 11 days and a quarter less than the Syriac year. This adds up to a difference of one year every 33 years. The Arab year ends without celebrating the *nawruz* [new year]. Before Islam, the Arabs added a supplementary month every three years. This they called Nasiʾ, meaning "deferment." God condemned this custom in verse 37 of sura 9: "Postponement (of a sacred month) is only an excess of disbelief. . . . " The Arabs established a regular order in their months: they began with Muharram, which is the first month of the year, and it is so called because throughout it war and all support for it are forbidden.[17]

The two interpretations are not necessarily contradictory, however. One can imagine, as often happens when political decision making gets muddled, that the tribesmen, who, keen on hunting and raiding, would not respect the respite of the *shahr haram* and would refuse to insert a Nasiʾ month every three years.

Islam gave to a disunited, disorderly people a means of taking hold of time and making use of the stars and their stations. Supremacy over earth is achieved through mastery of the heavens. If President Saddam Hussein had reread Tabari's introduction to his *Tarikh*, he would have quickly come to the conclusion that *al-zaman*, "time," in the elementary meaning of the succession of hours, belonged to Washington D.C. Even a strategist as limited as I would immediately conclude that if you want to "take the oil away from the Westerners and put it into the service of the Arabs and Muslims," you must first of all anchor your strategy in the heavens, with the beneficent and indispensable surveillance of the stars, real or artificial. This was obvious to our Prophet, who spent most of his time before the age of forty meditating on power and how to obtain it. As soon as you focus on determining the hour, day, or night, you immediately come to that conclusion. Without the help of the stars, a Muslim cannot go far. They are there to allow us to find our bearings and set our calendar. It is in such terms that Tabari explains the following verse 12 of sura 17:

> And we appoint the night and the day two portents. Then We make dark the portent of the night, and We make the portent of the day sight-giving, that ye may seek bounty from your Lord, and that ye may know the computation of the years, and the reckoning; and everything have We expounded with a clear expounding.

Great strategists guarantee the success of their armies by careful attention to apparently minor matters like the location of wells, the control of resupply and routes and passes, and especially the orchestration of operations according to a rigorously calculated time schedule. Apparently Saddam Hussein neglected one small detail that ended up assuring the success of his enemies—namely, that willy-nilly he was plugged into Coordinated Universal Time, a time that he was completely blind to, a time that is the prerogative of his enemies, who never undertake an act of war without "consulting the stars."

COORDINATED UNIVERSAL TIME

Like Saddam Hussein, Tabari, although born in the province of Tabaristan in 224/838, lived most of his life in Baghdad, where he taught theology and jurisprudence. In his era, establishing the time schedule for any activity that involved the community, whether it was the writing of a book of history or the conquest of new territory, was the first act to be undertaken. If Saddam Hussein had reacted as Tabari did more than a thousand years earlier and had begun his campaign by determining the time system that governed his action, he would have immediately realized the obvious: his time system is Coordinated Universal Time, which is dictated by Western satellites.

> Coordinated Universal Time (UTC), [the] international basis of civil and scientific time . . . is widely broadcast by precisely

140

coordinated radio signals; these radio time signals ultimately furnish the basis for the setting of all public and private clocks. UTC is obtained from atomic clocks, and the unit of UTC is the atomic second.[18]

Westerners, along with the Japanese, are the only ones in the world with a mastery of the technology necessary for setting up such a system: clocks synchronized at the global level through an interconnected satellite network minutely superimposed on what we think of as "the sky." According to Jacques Attali, "This extreme precision organizes a homogeneous time. . . . Therefore the planet lives on one single time."[19]

The Gulf War—that is, the destruction of Baghdad by teleguided, televised bombs—was so tragic for us Arabs and Muslims, whatever side we were on, because it made us aware that we are slaves of this Coordinated Universal Time that we have decided to ignore in order to keep a bit of dignity, in order not to acknowledge that we don't exist in our own time. We exist only in time defined by the West. We are exiles in Western time. The most horrible colonization is that which installs itself in your time, for there the wounds are to your dignity, and the resulting confusion borders on the pathological. "In two years the Japanese sold a million special timepieces destined for the Muslims. Marketed under the label *Kabir* (the greatest), they chime five times a day at the hour of prayer. A more expensive model recites a different Koranic verse at each hour."[20]

Nothing better illustrates the tragic decline of the Arabs than this Kabir watch (bought only by those who can afford it, those who share the oil income) because it epitomizes our trouble with identity. This tiny silicon chip, on which a holy calendar, cyclical by definition, is inscribed, is a technological device that denies the sacred vision of the cosmos and declaims the triumph of the electronic age, where profit is the be-all and end-all—the age of scientific man, who no longer fears death and draws power from his very mortality, for he has buried his gods long ago and reduced the earth and the stars to numbers processed by satellite, to the amount of material to be classified and consumed.

We Arabs and Muslims are exiled from this age, reduced to mere consumers of gadgets. This is one reason why the Arab and

Muslim masses and intellectuals poured into the streets in support of Iraq. It was not so much a wish to align themselves with Saddam Hussein as it was a condemnation of the buyers of Kabir watches and other gadgets, who waste the income from oil instead of using it to finance scientific development and to educate the young generation, now condemned to despair. And when you talk about Arab youth, you are talking about a demographic phenomenon without precedent in the world: "The annual mean rate of increase of the 0–24 age group is practically double that in the rest of the world." In the year 2000, 61 percent of the Arab population will fall in this age group, compared with only 48 percent of the world population.[21]

This generation of Arab youth, contrary to what one might think, is plugged in via television to what takes place in the West, for the satellite project that was to establish "an emancipated and emancipating community television" for the Arab world came to nothing.[22] Arabsat failed because the Arab governments didn't want television that was emancipating; they thought that when they had signed the contracts and paid the bills, they would gain yet another propaganda instrument to extoll their greatness, like the national television broadcasting that already exists. The Kabir syndrome is certainly well entrenched in those who manipulate decision making and petrodollars. But those who take the Arab masses for imbeciles forget that a people with a historical memory are difficult to "regiment." The artisans in the medina, literate or not, know about Harun al-Rashid's gift to Charlemagne. The caliph, a great patron of scientific development, offered its marvels to his peers:

In 807 Charlemagne received from Baghdad, as a gift from Harun al-Rashid, a brass water clock with moving figures, described in the Annals of Eginhard as similar to the Hercules clock at Gaza. A seventeenth-century text describes it thus: "A machine that, set in motion by the force of water, marks the hours by the appropriate number of little brass balls that fall on a brass bell. At noon twelve little horsemen emerge from twelve windows that close after them." This description, even though of a much later date, sounds credible, because the *Book of Knowledge of Ingenious Mechanical Devices* by Badi al-Zamanibal Ressa al-Tazari, written in the ninth century, establishes that such water clocks were known at that time in the whole Arab world.[23]

This memory is what saves us from decline and fall, for it gives us historical data that constantly put the present in perspective; musing about Harun al-Rashid focuses our frustrations on the quality of our leadership. Not that that worthy Abbasid caliph was a fiery partisan of democracy; he was on the contrary the architect of a most successful despotism. But he used the decision-making power he took from the people to carry out great scientific and economic projects. Modern despotism takes decision-making power from the people in order to buy Kabir watches from the Japanese.

Although Arab leaders have abandoned the Muslim calendar, it is still followed by the most dispossessed as a symbol of self-definition and commemorization. The tourist who has visited Morocco has surely had the experience of going shopping in the medina on a Friday and finding all the shops closed. And yet the official day of rest, for both the public and the private sectors, is Sunday. The mass of society, the millions of people who have never had access to modernity, who have been informally relegated to jobs where neither the minimum wage nor social benefits are guaranteed, ignore the official calendar and stick to the sacred calendar. It might be said that one of the manifestations of the class struggle in Morocco is the choice of calendar. The poorest live according to the Muslim calendar, while the richest live by the calendar of the West. Sometimes the calendars clash. The wealthy directors of the Rabat and Salé textile factories can never meet the fall delivery dates of their German customers because the underpaid and uninsured Moroccan factory workers take time off to participate in various celebrations and religious festivals to observe the Prophet's birthday, a holiday not marked on the German client's calendar in his office in Berlin. The workers leave for what is supposed to be a week, but if the holiday spirit and feeling of community solidarity of the dancing and religious chants for the celebration of the patron saint of Meknes are very exalting, they may extend the vacation for a second week.

The struggle over the calendar is also an intergenerational struggle. Although some of the young opt for fundamentalism, growing beards and spending time in the mosques, many sing Hit Parade songs at the top of their lungs and dream more of *Kojak* and *Dallas* than of Harun al-Rashid. For these young people, their frustrations cultivated by television, the Muslim calendar is becoming a fuzzy reference point. Our tragedy is that our calendar more and more determines just religious rituals and holidays. In the majority of Arab countries, on the eve of the first day of the Muslim year, the first of Muharram, young people go to bed early, whereas on December 31 we have trouble getting to sleep before dawn. Auto horns and teenage songs blare away, accompanied by local or international radio stations broadcasting the latest American hits.

Our whole life—the production of goods and services, political and economic decision making, the circulation of people and ideas, the banks, the airports—runs on Coordinated Time, omitting the euphemistic "universal." Since we are forced to live according to the Western calendar, our calendar now marks just the time of prayer, which still serves to anchor the life of the humble believer to the trajectory of the stars. Otherwise why do the five daily prayers bear the names of the positions of the sun in the sky? The prayers are a way of putting the believer in orbit, since he keeps constant watch on the sun to know the time of prayer: the first is called *al-fajr* (dawn); the second is *duha* (midday); the third, *'asr*, marks the beginning of the sun's descent; the fourth, *maghrib*, is at sundown; and finally the last, *'asha*, announces the night.

We no longer live according to the rhythm of the sacred calendar, but we have not succeeded in creating the technological base that alone would guarantee access to the *kawn* (cosmos), the highest stake in the power game. Disconnected from our Muslim calendar, we are even more disconnected from the electronic calendar, that of Coordinated Time. This double disconnection gives our otherwise luminous days a twilight look. How often am I asked by young students, "*Ustada* [professor], what is going to happen to us? Why does our work have no value? Why is our life so absurd?" How, except to lower one's eyes and break off the conversation, can one respond to those faces, so full of hope and innocence, reflecting a belief in the wisdom of their elders?

144

Renaming the moon *qamar* is certainly not the answer, as the fundamentalists sadly call for. Going back to year 1 of the Hejira is only important in that it lets us grasp the essential point: Islam's beautiful gift to the Arabs, which was to teach them to lift their heads, in the most basic meaning of the expression. It taught us to walk through life with eyes fixed on the sun and the stars, that is, intimately connected to the cosmos and conscious of being a part of it. It is that galactic tradition of Islam that should be reactivated as the basic movement for our development, for it is in line with the planetary outlook that technology both permits and encourages. The difference between an Arab of the *jahiliyya* and a Muslim Arab, after year 1 of the calendar, is that the attention of the former was on the tribe that had two camels more than his tribe—camels he intended to steal—whereas the focus of the latter was on the stars. It was this cosmic focus that almost immediately gave meaning and power to life. The loss of the cosmic dimension is what has caused our confusion about our identity, creating trouble for us in living the present, which is nothing but absurdity and debacle, because our actions lead to nothing. The dance around the stars, the celebration of science and technology, is not universal. It is a tribal dance around the American flag.

NONUNIVERSAL MODERNITY: ARMSTRONG'S FLAG

The feeling of absurdity that pervades our lives today stems from the fact that modernity reminds us every minute that it is Western, and that since that night of July 20, 1969, when a tall blond man planted the flag of his nation on it, the moon is not universal. That tall blond man was named Neil Armstrong, and he was an American. We were happy to witness that triumph of the scientific spirit, that extraordinary breakthrough toward reaching the stars. But we were called back to reality by the astronaut's flag, which did not celebrate the universal but rather was the flag of his tribe, as was astutely pointed out by the late mythologist Joseph Campbell: "And then, as though immediately at home there, two astronauts in their space suits were to be seen moving about in a dream-landscape, performing their assigned tasks, setting up the American flag."[24] Many Americans swelled with pride at this event, but those who thought about the responsibility of their country to establish universalism, in which everyone is welcome—those like Campbell, who as a student of myth analyzed the survival and dangerous metamorphoses of the archaic—were shocked by this primitive act.

Following the planting of the American flag, non-Western spectators were treated to a quotation from the Bible. The Apollo astronauts who came before Armstrong and were the first to orbit the moon carried one in their space suits and recited before the television camera from the first chapter of Genesis: "In the beginning God created the heaven and the earth. And the earth was without form, and void; and darkness was upon the face of the deep. . . . " "How sad, I thought," concludes Campbell, "that we should have had nothing in our own poetry to match the sense of that prodigious occasion! Nothing to match, or even to suggest, the marvel and the magnitude of the universe into which we then were moving!"[25]

It is a given that the West, which flaunts before us the dream of one world, bears responsibility for the future of humanity. Its responsibility is heavy because it holds a quasi-monopoly on decision making in matters of science and technology. It alone decides if satellites will be used to educate Arabs or to drop bombs on them. It is understandable and even excusable that the Third World, off course and unable to participate in the celebration of science, seeks to find its way by drawing on myths and historical memory. But when the West, which is opening the way toward the galactic era, trots out tribal flags and Bibles to inaugurate man's exploration of the moon, it does not help the excluded, among them Arab youth, feel they are partners in this universality.

It is obvious that the powerful, monolithic West that haunts our Arab imagination is more fiction than fact, especially in the decade of the nineties, since the fall of the Berlin Wall. Torn by ethnic and regional rivalries, it is disintegrating before our eyes. Nevertheless, for us Arabs this West, splintering into a myriad of conflicting interests, still has power over our daily lives. It crushes our potentialities and invades our lives with its imported products and televised movies that swamp the airwaves. Seen from the Arab side of the Mediterranean, the West (more exactly, Europe), however

146

splintered and divided it may be, is a power that crushes us, besieges our markets, and controls our merest resources, initiatives, and potentialities. This was how we perceived our situation, and the Gulf War turned our perception into certitude. The pertinent question we have to ask, then, is, Does the West have the power to create a universal culture? Westerners might retort that forming a universal culture is everybody's concern. I believe that forming a universal culture is the concern of those who hold the monopolies, especially the monopoly of knowledge, and that the responsibility of the West is extremely great. The West can surely produce a universal culture if it renounces its monopoly on scientific knowledge and the electronic agenda. The West can create a universal culture if it renounces its flags.

Equal sharing and the access of all to this knowledge is not a utopian dream. It is written into the very nature of electronic technology, which is nothing but communication and circulation of information. "By definition, both force and wealth," says Alvin Toffler, "are the property of the strong and the rich. It is the truly revolutionary characteristic of knowledge that it can be grasped by the poor and weak as well. So it is the most democratic of the sources of power."[26]

The West can revoke the challenge it poses to human history by operating according to its own archaisms, and the best way to do so would be to include others in its decision making. It could begin by tapping the talents of the thousands of Third World intellectuals and savants who live in the West, often as political exiles, who are rarely invited to participate in fashioning the Western approach to the subject of universality. They could become a bridge between the very powerful and baffling West and those other cultures with their complex wishes for both change and stability, their overtures and rejections, their hesitations and retreats.

The fate of women depends in large measure on such an adoption of responsibility on the part of the West, for, paradoxical as it may seem, it is these women, veiled and immobilized by tradition, who have been metamorphosed by modernity into Egerias of freedom. It is they who sing loudest of individualism, for they, more than anyone else, were suppressed by the law of the group. Condemned for so long to silence, their song rhymes "liberty" with "individuality," introducing strange music into the city. They are fascinating and frightening; they arouse anger and they are defiant. The imams condemn them, but they stand firm. Without masks, frail and with faces uncovered, they are starting their forward march, without supervision for the first time, in a city where all holds fast except the boundaries.

10

Women's Song: Destination Freedom

The Arab world is about to take off.

This is not a prophecy. It is a woman's intuition, and God, who knows everything, knows that women's intuition is rarely wrong.

It is going to take off for the simple reason that everybody, with the fundamentalists in the lead, wants change. The fact that they propose to go forward by going backward doesn't alter the fact that they ardently want change. There is a very strong wish in this corner of the world to go elsewhere, to migrate collectively to another present. Foreigners perhaps do not feel this, but every morning I wake up with the radio at my ear and think: anything can happen; perhaps everything will change between one minute and the next.

By plunging a knife into the sore spots—dependence, lack of democracy, powerlessness—the Gulf War shattered something deep within us. I have thought a lot about what that might be, and I have come to the conclusion that it smashed the multiple circles of cold fear that have pressed on us. What worse could happen to Arabs than what the war produced—the whole West with all its technology dropping bombs on us? It was the ultimate horror. When you have gone through an experience of horror—and all those who have experienced deep depression know it—you emerge free of fear. Not that you are rid of it, but you have conquered it. The Arab world, paralyzed by all the fears that this book explores, has finally with this war had the opportunity to live through them and emerge from the experience, a bit shaky perhaps, but with the firm conviction that making the perilous jump into the unknown is the least dangerous thing that could happen to us.

A sense of hurtling toward the unknown is already reflected in good-natured daily chitchat: "*Ma zal 'ayish?*" ("Are you still alive?") replaced "Hi, how are you?" during the war. Everyone now knows that for an Arab, surviving means changing, exploring those dimensions of life that have been muzzled—*'aql* (reason), individual freedom, *ra'y* (judgment), and especially *khayal,* that power of imagination that will assure supremacy in the world of the future. But although Arabs are amazed in this post-Gulf War era at the possibilities opening up to them, women already began their resolute and perilous march toward the realm of freedom some decades ago. Why, I will be asked, did women form this audacious avant-garde? Because we had nothing to lose except our fears, our masks, and all the crippling effects of segregation and confinement.

Women are eager to plunge into adventure and the unknown. The symbol of that eagerness is the Palestinian Mother Courage whom we see every day on our television screens, standing firmly in the street, neither intimidated nor filled with hatred toward the Israeli soldiers whom she scolds as though they were teenagers who have trouble relinquishing adolescence to become adults.

Arab women are not afraid of modernity, because for them it is an unhoped-for opportunity to construct an alternative to the tradition that weighs so heavily on them. They long to find new worlds where freedom is possible. For centuries, confined and masked, they have been singing about freedom, but no one was listening. Muhammad al-Fasi, a Moroccan scholar, had the idea of collecting some of the songs that circulated in the harems of Fez during the 1930s. Many spoke of forbidden passions, of nocturnal rendezvous, of crazy escapades, and some ridiculed the effectiveness of locks and chains. Others celebrated the bird who played false when given the chance:

Tir! al-tir!
Bnit lu shabak hrir
Ma nwit ytir
Ba'd ma wallaf.

Birdie! Birdie!
To keep it I built a cage of silk
And never thought it would fly away
After letting itself be tamed.[1]

Women never let themselves be tamed. Men believed that a person could become accustomed to confinement. But women were waiting for the right moment, the moment of difference with dignity, of participation and dialogue, and that moment has arrived.

THEY HAVE ALREADY LEFT, AND THE IMAMS ARE WORRIED

Women have already taken flight.

Pale and grave, they are performing the pilgrimage that their grandmothers dreamed of for so long: to dance without a mask, with eyes riveted on a limitless horizon.

They are afraid, they stumble and feel weak—how do you move about when chains were your programmed destiny? But the call of the open sea is irresistible.

They fall down and get up again; they educate themselves and kick over the traces. How can you roam when a cage was to be your future?

At the beginning, both frightened and frightening, they petrified men. Then, as the years rolled by, the men, recovered from their consternation, began to listen to the women who were singing about roaming and were longing for the obliteration of boundaries. Such a strange song it was, seeming to mistake itself for that symphony of the universal that the foreign West was intoning like a hymn to the galaxies. Harems exist anymore only on postcards or in the palaces of a few emirs who have enough money to re-create a gimcrack version of those of Baghdad of the Golden Age. The rest of the men are beginning to feel almost at home in this apocalyptic renaissance where power is to be found in moving forward and not in the past. According to the Syrian poet Adonis, in the abyss that modernity represents, the Arab man must change and

151

rethink himself in cosmic terms, including the possibility of being as nebulous as the wind:

> He comes defenseless like the forest,
> And like a cloud he cannot be held back.
> Yesterday he carried a continent
> And moved the sea.
> Uncertainty is his country,
> But his eyes are numberless.
> He strides into the abyss
> And is like the wind.[2]

Arab women do not always say what they are thinking, but these men who are striding into the abyss and are like the wind are more than ever the lovers of whom they have dreamed—nomads of modernity, traveling light, seeking no country, for moving forward is their tribe.

It is not true that our mothers were happy with our fathers, wrapped in their own certitudes. My uncle Hajj Muhammad would overturn the table and threaten to pronounce the formula of repudiation every time Aunt Kanza put a little too much salt or pepper in the couscous on Fridays. She wept on the day of his death, and she keeps his memory alive and nurses it, but did she love him? Can you love a man who is always right because the law binds the wife to marital obedience? Everyone knows that men who are uncertain of themselves, who are feeling their way, are the most attractive. Young Arabs know it, and love affairs are only the better for it. What is certain is that women have decided to listen no longer to *khutaba* (sermons) they have not had a hand in writing. They are ready for takeoff. They have always known that the future rests on the abolition of boundaries, that the individual is born to be respected, that difference is enriching. For them, the San Francisco charter is neither a novelty nor a breakthrough. It is just the formulation of a dream that losers have always cherished, like a talisman that protects them.

Meanwhile the imams, who have proclaimed for centuries that marital *ta'a* (obedience) is a duty, are fuming. Obeying the husband means obeying God. The word *ta'a*, which appears in contemporary civil codes, reproduces in the harem blind obedience to the caliph. The imams are irate because if domestic *ta'a* is challenged by weak women, how can men be expected to lower their eyes in deference to the leader? The modesty of the Arab woman is the linchpin of the whole political system. Entire chapters in the collections of Hadith (sayings and actions of the Prophet) dictate to us how to braid our hair, how to lower our eyes, and how to slip on modesty like a camisole. The sermons continue today. A new book on the dangers of mixing the sexes, published at great expense in Cairo, offers to the believer for 95 dirhams ($10) a seven-hundred-page tome, "Dress and Adornment: The Purifying Tradition,"[3] whose author has collected all that the *fiqh* (religious knowledge) orders women to do regarding such crucial questions as how to wear the *sarwal,* the wide-legged pantaloon so common in the Muslim world, how to pluck the eyebrows and depilate the skin, and the rights and wrongs of wearing rouge, and finally includes a very important chapter on footwear. No, certainly not all men are ready for takeoff, for the journey toward uncertainties, toward plural modernities, toward cities without protection, because they get paid too much oil money for preserving the benefits of the *hijab* and the virtues of obedience.

The ancestral violence against those who refuse to obey is being mobilized this time not against the Mu'tazila or the Sufis, long buried, but against those who have taken up their chant, women who want a city without ramparts, where children blossom in the abode of change and find their roots in the only traditions that are still valid, those of the odyssey of the stars.

As for the violence in the ancestral cities, it was women who were its most quiet victims and most silent scapegoats. The caliphs never respected them. From the moment any crisis began, it was women and wine that were condemned. For centuries women and wine were regarded as the source of all our troubles.

THE CALIPHATE AND WOMEN: CRISIS AND VIOLENCE

Banning mixing of the sexes and advocating the separation of men and women as the measure to alleviate all political crises is far from

153

being a novelty in Muslim political history. It is a tradition, even a state tradition. Opposition forces claim past practice as the basis for treating women with contempt. A Muslim sovereign in a crisis, facing hunger riots or a popular revolt, immediately has recourse to the traditional measures of destroying the stores of wine and placing a ban on women leaving their homes, and especially on their using the same means of transportation as men, reducing them to a state of immobility in capitals like Cairo and Baghdad which are traversed by great rivers. Wine and women—here we have the Gordian knot of the crisis. *Tathir,* the ritual purification of the social body, requires the destruction of the first and the confinement of the second. The recent violence against women which we have seen in Algeria, like the burning of the house of a feminist activist in Annaba on November 15, 1989, is in the purest caliphal tradition.

Al-Hakim, the Fatimid caliph who ordered his mathematician to regulate the waters of the Nile, turned to other, more realizable, measures to calm the masses when the waters continued to fall and the failure of crops provoked enormous inflation.[4] In year 405 of the Hejira he decided to act, ordering Egyptian women to be shut in: "In that year al-Hakim forbade women to leave their houses at all; he forbade them to go to the public baths and put an end to manufacture of shoes for women. Many opposed his orders and were killed."[5]

Some decades later, in year 487, a similar scene took place in Baghdad. The caliph al-Muqtadi, the twenty-eighth ruler of the Abbasid dynasty, exiled women singers and women of ill fame from the city: "Their houses were sold and they themselves sent into exile; people were forbidden to go to the public baths without a *mi'zar* [loincloth]. . . . Sailors were also forbidden to transport men and women together."[6] When the anger of a prince against women abated but the populace was still tormented by economic insecurity, the measures against women were often made part of a "package" of prohibitions. These prohibitions, such as banning certain food and drinks, as futile as they were bothersome, introduced into the city the thing that frightens Muslims the most: the making violence banal. The link in historical memory between crisis, calamity, and *tathir* is very strong and has persisted throughout the centuries, right up to the present. Shaykh ʿAbbas Madani, one of the leaders of the Algerian fundamentalist movement, is convinced that it is women and wine that are at the bottom of the economic and political troubles that are shaking his country:

> Our religion enjoins us to take counsel. The Prophet, may health be his, said: "Religion is counsel". . . . So we have tried in all circumstances to consult with our brothers, to work together for the well-being of this community and this country. . . . We have seen moral calamities that have no connection with religion or with the traditions of the Algerian. Consumption of wine has become legal; mixing of the sexes in schools, lycées, and universities has led to the proliferation of bastards. Depravity has spread, and we see that women no longer cover themselves but display their bodies with makeup and naked for all to see both indoors and outdoors. Where then is the dignity of the Algerian man after his honor has been publicly flouted?[7]

The reform program of a leader who makes this kind of analysis of his nation's problems is very simple: box women in and ban wine!

Curtailing women's freedom to move about, thus immobilizing half of the *umma,* far from being a negative, fits in comfortably with any Muslim sovereign's reform measures. This theory of crisis and crisis solutions constantly recurs in Muslim history in the Muslim West and in the East. According to al-Murakushi, one of the most brilliant historians of the thirteenth century, women's emergence into the streets and onto the political scene destroyed the powerful Berber dynasty of the Almoravids, whose western empire extended from Spain to North Africa. Al-Murakushi depicts the last sovereign of the dynasty as powerless before the rising tide of religious opponents, who proposed like the fundamentalists of today that the state adopt a policy of conformity and unity. They were called *al-muwahhidin* (those who unify). Animosity toward women was a key part of their propaganda. Al-Murakushi summarizes the crisis thus:

155

The situation of the Commander of the Faithful grew very shaky around the year 500 [of the Hejira]. The *manakir* [sins] increased in number. This happened because the important persons of the dynasty behaved like despots . . . women took charge of public affairs; they were given power. . . . Andalusia was in a state of revolt and threatened to return to its previous state [that is, to Christianity].[8]

The Almoravids, who were from the Sahara, where nomadic life still gives women a prominent role in the survival of the group, had a more respectful attitude toward women. These Almoravid women, like Zainab, the wife of Yusif Ibn Tashfin, the founder of the dynasty, played an important part in politics.

Seven centuries later, in the middle of the twentieth century, the extraordinary writer Ahmad Amin, author of the trilogy *Fajr al-Islam* (Dawn of Islam), *Duha al-Islam* (Morning of Islam), and *Zuhr al-Islam* (High Noon of Islam), a monumental attempt to synthesize fifteen hundred years of history, repeats the same refrain, maintaining that time and again women have been the gravediggers of dynasties: from the moment they became visible in society, the dynasty and Muslim order foundered. The fundamentalist opposition movements that extol the veil are reactivating this age-old connection.

It is these centuries of misogyny, cultivated as tradition in the corridors of caliphal despotism, that Muslim women are now challenging. They are compelling the faithful, baffled by the cosmic changes that assail them from every direction, to do what just three decades ago was considered utterly farcical: to regard women as equals. They are demanding the renunciation of the ideal of the homogeneous city, carefully divided into two hierarchical spaces, where only one sex manages politics and monopolizes decision making. The emergence of women means the emergence of the stranger within the city. It means a painful but necessary learning process for the majority in a society where *al-hisn,* "the citadel," which supervises and controls, is still the law. *Al-muhsana* is one of the legal terms for a married woman; she is protected by her marriage, which is like a *hisn.* The civil codes reproduce in every article the picture of a family in the image of the caliphal palace, where *ta'a* is required and the will of the leader overrides that of all others.

The battle of the 1990s will be a battle over the civil codes, which women challenge as contrary to the Universal Declaration of Human Rights, and which the authoritarian states defend as sacred. By propelling women out of the house into the streets through education and paid work, modernity has perverted the ideal homogeneous city, pushing it into dangerous territory where unmasked, irreverent women speak an unknown language. The equality they demand, say the supporters of caliphal, despotic Islam, is a foreign, imported idea. These women are traitors, allies of the West and its philosophies, like the Mu'tazila and rationalists of yesteryear who tried to import Greek ideas.

Women have been, are, and will continue to be the targets of intimidation and violence, whether from regimes in power or opposition movements that hark back to the past. It happened in Pakistan in the 1980s; it is still going on in Iran; and today, at the beginning of the 1990s, it is happening in Algeria. Tomorrow the same thing can happen elsewhere. The reason is simple: women are the only ones who publicly assert their right to self-affirmation as individuals, and not just through words but also through actions (e.g., unveiling and going out).[9] Today they constitute one of the most dynamic components of the developing civil society. Although up to the present they are still politically unorganized, they have succeeded in infiltrating one of the citadels which was long forbidden to them: formal education. Education, with high school and university diplomas, is women's new acquisition. Until now all that women were taught to do, from housework to carpet weaving, was devalued and poorly paid.

A FORCE FOR RADICAL CHALLENGE

One thing that the West, always fascinated by the veiled woman,[10] knows little of and the imams know only too well, is that women are certainly no longer cooped up in harems, nor are they veiled and silent. They have massively infiltrated forbidden territory, notably the universities. If in Iran the imams keep close watch on women, it is because women constituted 19 percent of the teaching staff of universities in 1986, while the rate in West Germany for the same year was 17 percent.[11] There is no other explanation for the fact that one of the first acts of Imam Khomeini as chief of state in 1980 was to promulgate the law on the *hijab,* making the veil obligatory for women who worked in government institutions.[12] The relentless battle of the fundamentalists, whether in the government or the opposition, doesn't target just any woman. One precise category is aimed at: middle-class women who have had access to education and valorizing salaried jobs. The enemy to be fought is not the female proletariat, the women wearing the traditional djellaba, who are worn out by long bus trips (which they often must take at night in order to be on time) to and from work, and who are underpaid and without union protection. This proletariat interests neither the opposition forces nor the regimes based on the sacred. Their obsession is with the woman who enjoys and exercises all the visible privileges of her modernity: she is bareheaded, with windblown hair, she drives a car, and she has identity papers and a passport in her own name in her handbag. The woman who is so disturbing is not she who is content just to be listed on the family register, who allows her husband to vote for her; rather, it is she who has gained legitimate access to the university and, from the height of her new academic *minbar* (mosque pulpit), preaches, writes, educates, and protests. It is she who is the target of the fundamentalists, from the most princely to the most popular.

It was women like this who organized the Women's Action Forum and went into the streets to agitate against the military regime of Zia al-Haq in Pakistan. It was university women like these who surged into the streets in front of the presidential palace in Algiers to demand democracy. They were the first to unmask the despotism behind the socialism of the FLN (National Liberation Front), which under the burnous of chivalry was posing as "revolutionary fighter." Proletarian women may not be participating in such protests, but their burdens are heavier to bear, what with their many children and the lack of child-care facilities, as well as the long waiting lines for buses. They come along when they can, but it is certainly not they who constitute the leaders. In both cases, that of Pakistan and Algeria, women went into the streets in the last decade to challenge the *shari'a* as administered by officialdom, risking being condemned as infidels. And in both cases the leaders of the movements are none other than university graduates who in 1984 were already more than 25 percent of the teachers in higher education in Pakistan and 24 percent in Algeria.[13]

To understand the intensity of today's violent feelings against the desire of women to liberate themselves, we must recall the keenness with which women threw themselves into education, like drowning persons into an unhoped-for lifeboat. In less than two generations, since the Second World War, they have laid siege to the academic world. The modern university has been more welcoming and less hostile to women. Recognition should be given to the crucial role played by progressive intellectuals, who were the first to help and support them. Contrary to what one might think, the progressive Arab man has always seen the problem of his relationship to women as central to his desire for change; in Morocco the men of the Left were women's accomplices and confidants in their struggle. Thanks to them, things began to change and the university became a place of hope. For women of my generation higher education was regarded not as a luxury, but as a chance for survival and escape from the widespread contempt for women that characterized the traditional ordering of society a few decades ago. In the 1960s women could neither engage in business nor launch political careers. Only the university and education provided a legitimate way out of mediocrity. Women did not study to be nurses or nurse's aides; subordinate jobs re-created the domestic scene. Therefore the aim was medical school. In 1987 50 percent of all medical students in Tunisia were women, 37 percent in Syria, and 30 percent in Algeria.[14]

The rapidity of change in intersex relations was dizzying if we take access to the university as the index. In Japan, that other traditional and very conservative society, despite the push into the scientific and technological domain after World War II, by 1987 only 10 percent of university professors were women. Even in Egypt, where the virulent fundamentalism of the Muslim Brotherhood is equaled only by the agitation of Egyptian feminists, it was

159

28 percent in 1986, higher than in the United States (24 percent in 1980) and France (23 percent in 1987).[15]

Fundamentalism was born in Egypt at the same time as feminism, and the two have never ceased to exist side by side. For a North African like me, whose mother was illiterate, attending conferences in Egypt is always a renewed surprise: the heroines of feminism are not young things in miniskirts. They are women the age of grandmothers, gray-haired and with quavering voices, but whose remarks are full of vitriol. The Ikhwan al-Muslimin, the Muslim Brotherhood, came into being in the years 1928 to 1936. At that same time, the Egyptian feminist Huda Shaʿrawi was between 1923 and 1947 (the date of her death) the leader of one of the most radical feminist movements in the world, even by today's standards, a movement that asserted respect for the individual as its basic article of faith.[16] In 1920 Egyptian women had already created an important section within the Wafd party and had gained the support of a significant segment of public opinion.

The animosity of the fundamentalists toward feminists in the Arab world is due to the fact that there are two groups that have profited from modern education: men from the countryside and lower classes, and city women of the middle and upper classes. These two groups make up the new middle class that was created in recent decades through free state education. Conflict between the two is natural; it is one of the new forms of class struggle that has developed in the very dynamic Arab world. The interests of these two groups are different, and it is to be expected that each struggles to impose its world vision. The problem is that the fundamentalists act with the complicity of the state, while women struggle alone, with no protection even from the divine—for the fundamentalists claim a monopoly on speaking in the name of God. What we are seeing today is a claim by women to their right to God and the historical tradition. This takes various forms. There are women who are active within the fundamentalist movements and those who work on a reinterpretation of the Muslim heritage as a necessary ingredient of our modernity. Our liberation will come through a rereading of our past and a reappropriation of all that has structured our civilization. The mosque and the Koran

160

belong to women as much as do the heavenly bodies. We have a right to all of that, to all its riches for constructing our modern identity.

Reducing women fundamentalists to obedient bystanders is to badly misunderstand the dynamics of the religious protest movement. We have seen the importance of concepts like *haqq* (right) and *'adl* (justice). Even if at the beginning women recruits were there to be manipulated, in many Muslim countries today—for instance, Iran and Algeria—we see the emergence of a virulent feminist leadership within the fundamentalist parties. We don't have to fall victim to stereotyping. We must remain vigilant and keep open, analytical minds, as have the Iranian sociologist Nayereh Tohidi and the whole group of women experts who recently attended the conference "Identity, Politics, and Women." Their conclusion was that even within the ranks of the fundamentalists, feminist challenge is emerging and causing surprises.[17]

Parallel to their access to the academic worlds, Arab women in general and Egyptian women in particular (first within the nationalist movement and later as independent voices, like Huda Sha'rawi) energized a feminist movement inundating the press with pamphlets and articles and profoundly changed attitudes.[18] We probably owe to them the speeded-up decision to grant women the right to vote and the statement of the rights to education and work which was inserted in the first draft of the Charter of the Arab League in the 1940s. During the 1970s the Egyptian Nawal El Saadawi played an important role as the first to open discussion among Arabs about authoritarian relationships and about sexuality as the special domain of violence. Millions of young people devoured books by these feminists. Although they were of course banned, this only increased the demand for them and taught us to practice the politics of the "tireless pen"—that is, the more the police ban, the more must be written. When a woman's work is censored, she must not let herself be discouraged. Instead of writing five pages a day, she must produce six or even seven. The objective is to overwhelm the censor with the amount of reading he has to do to "keep up." Frequent imprisonment by various regimes did not daunt the courage of Nawal. The journal she edited,

Nun, and the association she organized, Solidarity of Arab Women, have both recently been banned, the first before the Gulf War and the second just after.

The great surprise of the 1980s, however, comes from Saudi women. Despite the strengthening of surveillance and the almost prisonlike atmosphere in which they live, many have succeeded just since the 1970s in getting university degrees. In Saudi Arabia, 32 percent of university professors in 1986 were women.[19] The universities, of course, are segregated, but that hasn't stopped Saudi women from hiding beneath their veils doctoral degrees from great academic institutions, often British or American. A woman with a doctorate, even though she is still condemned in Saudi Arabia to the veil and seclusion, is not like an illiterate woman relegated to the kitchen. Modern education introduces a new dimension and changes the authority relationship between a woman and her group. This is the only explanation for the outcry of the imams against the handful of Saudi women who broke the ban on driving and drove around the streets of Riyadh at the wheel of their cars during the Gulf War.

Although women have succeeded in entering all kinds of professions, it is their presence in the domain of the university which has allowed them, given the very nature of the profession, to devote free time to research and writing. The impact of women writers, as journalists, editors of journals, authors, and especially novelists and playwrights, is enormous.[20] Unlike what I hear in publishing circles in the West, feminist literature and books written by women sell very well, and the majority of the buyers are men. The Arab world values women's writing, and many women novelists appear year after year on the best-seller lists. The books of novelists and essayists like the Egyptian Salwa Bakr, the Palestinian Liana Badr, and the Lebanese Ghada al-Sammam and Hanane el-Cheikh, and of poets like the Kuwaiti Su'ad al-Sabbah and the Syrian Hamida Na'na'—to name just a few—are always available in kiosks and compete well throughout the Arab world with the "oil culture," the made-to-order conservative propaganda. The journal *Shahrazad,* whose editor is the Libyan Fatima Mahmud, and which is published in Cyprus and distributed throughout the Arab world, gives its readers the sharpest analysis of the conflict between women and the conservative forces.[21] While debate on the woman question in the journals of the Left is still the prisoner of endless ideological debates and stilted language, these writers' clear style, their simple, direct exposition of what is wrong and what needs changing, and their lack of pretention counts for much in women's success.

The call for the return to the *hijab* which intensified during the 1980s is a reaction to women's activity and agitation on the cultural front. The animosity of the conservative forces must be seen within the context of the dissemination of these women's works in a society that is accustomed to the idea that the illiteracy of women is traditional. The religious authorities, who were very active during the nationalist struggle, rested on their laurels after independence. But they were suddenly startled awake in the last decade by the most salacious, monstrous *gharib* (stranger) ever seen or heard: an educated woman, unveiled, agitating in the street in the name of the Charter of the United Nations and against the *shariʿa* of officialdom.

Aswat al-gharb (voices of the West) is how the conservatives label this phenomenon: alien forces are here among us, in the city. Women take off the veil, and what is seen? A *gharib* face, strange like the West. The result is that they are nonplussed and confused. One of my colleagues, who likes me very much, after fifteen years of working side by side with me at the Université Mohammed V, has still not succeeded in accepting me as a local; he always calls me Fatima Swidiyya (Fatima the Swede), even in August when, after months at the beach, I am black as an olive. The "monstrousness" of the modern woman, as compared to the traditional model, lies not so much in her access to knowledge as in her claim to be a citizen, challenging the government by referring to the United Nations Charter and the Universal Declaration of Human Rights. Educated women have always existed in the Muslim world, especially in the upper classes, where they often specialized in the study and teaching of religious texts. ʿUmar Kahhala devoted a large part of his four-volume work on famous Arab and Muslim women to them.[22] Female illiteracy, even in the well-off classes, is one of the characteristics of the decadence that led to colonization.[23] What is new today and constitutes a break with the past is that women are posing their challenge as a problem between them and the state, a contract to be renegotiated. This is certainly a fundamental revolution. Traditionally the state ignores women, except in times of crisis, when it fiercely attacks them.

Muslim women do not have a government that protects them. This is the basis of their tragedy during this very slow transition from the despotic medieval state to the modern state. For them, the modern state has still not yet been born. They are battling by themselves, and all the violence against them, beginning with that of the government, is permitted and even legitimized since the personal status laws make inequality a sacred matter. This explains the insistence of the Algerian fundamentalists on proxy voting, which has permitted them to vote on behalf of their wives during recent municipal elections.[24] Modernity means the emergence of women as citizens, and this emergence suddenly transforms the nature of the state. The worst danger women face is unemployment, which threatens to engulf them in the coming decade. What will be the effect of the Gulf War on women's chances to negotiate democratic relationships, and what is the responsibility of the West as victor in the region and the dominant power in its new economy, in Mr. Bush's New World Order?

THE EFFECT OF THE GULF WAR ON WOMEN: UNEMPLOYMENT, OIL, AND THE *HIJAB*

Unemployment is the gravest threat to stability in the Arab states. One of its causes is the annual rate of population increase—one of the highest in the world, 3.9 percent. From 1985 to 1990, the Arab population increased from 188 million to 217 million. It grew by 29 million in just five years! It is predicted that between 1990 and 2000 there will be an increase of 64 million, putting the Arab population at 281 million by the end of the century.[25]

Women, as half this population, (108 million in 1990, almost equal to the population of France and western Germany combined)—most of whom are under twenty-five years of age—represent a large army of job seekers. Already in 1990, two Arabs out of three were twenty-four years old and under.[26] This group numbers

167.5 million, of whom half are adolescents. When we talk about Arab women, therefore, we are not talking about mature, settled women; we are talking about *83 million job seekers* who will marry late because, like young men, they are concerned about their futures and want to get an education first. Whereas early marriage used to be the rule, today the Arab world is seeing a spectacular delay in the age of marriage,[27] and since this trend was neither anticipated nor codified, there has been an increase in out-of-wedlock births. The Algerian leader Shaykh Madani, who is a sociologist, knows the statistics well. By calling for the return to the *hijab,* the fundamentalists delegitimize the presence of women on the labor market. It is an extraordinarily powerful political weapon.

The *hijab* is manna from heaven for politicians facing crises. It is not just a scrap of cloth; it is a division of labor. It sends women back to the kitchen. *Any Muslim state can reduce its level of unemployment by half just by appealing to the* sharicа, *in its meaning as despotic caliphal tradition.* This is why it is important to avoid reducing fundamentalism to a handful of agitators who stage demonstrations in the streets. It must be situated within its regional and world economic context by linking it to the question of oil wealth and the New World Order that the Westerners propose to us.

The West came out of the Gulf War a winner, but along with it Saudi Arabia, the most conservative regime in the Arab world and the one most contemptuous of human rights, emerged not only stronger but also more than ever the determining power for our future. Two-thirds of the world's oil reserves still sleep quietly beneath the soil of Mecca. It is normal that millions of unemployed Arabs dream of a more favorable distribution of this wealth as a solution to their problems. In parallel with what the Lebanese writer George Corm calls "the irresistible rise of oil tyranny," Saudi Arabia has inundated these millions of unemployed with Islamic propaganda, whose concepts of *haqq* and *cadala* constitute an explosive force that so well expresses their feelings of frustration.[28]

The role of oil in fundamentalism should never be forgotten. The resistance to progressive ideas, financed in large measure by the Saudi oil money that was simultaneously producing an extravagant, princely Islamic culture, gave birth to a rigid authoritarianism closed to *rahma*. A better term for fundamentalism in Saudi Arabia would be petro-Wahhabism, whose pillar is the veiled woman.[29]

The lining up of the North African masses against the bombing of Iraq is explained in part by their hostility toward the Saudi regime. This regime, insofar as it is a key piece on the world chessboard, is seen as incapable of managing its oil wealth to create full employment in the region. The Gulf War put a finger on the problem: the absence of democracy, which results in this wealth being managed as a monopoly by a few families. The news reports during the war about the sums paid by Kuwait to the government of President Mitterand to help it get through the crisis were received and commented on in the medinas as the most unjust absurdity, strengthening more than ever the conviction that full employment could be achieved only by democratization of the Arab states.

This war without frontiers has inaugurated the era of responsibility without frontiers. From now on, Arab youths know that the hand cut off in Saudi Arabia can no longer be blamed solely on the Saudi regime, which revealed its weakness during the conflict. Above all, they know that it is not Islam that demands such horrors, but an anachronistic regime that can hide its archaisms only by veiling them with the sacred. At last Islam is no longer guilty of what happens in Saudi Arabia in this New World Order that Mr. Bush urges on us. The American president has taken on ethical responsibility for the region, and along with him François Mitterand and Helmut Kohl and the citizens who elected them in the representative democracies of the West. Whoever consumes Arab oil is responsible.

Paradoxically, the Gulf War showed that oil, which was the basis for this conflict and which up to the present has set off the incessant hostilities that have plagued the area, can bring cultures together and sharpen the sense of responsibility. The West needs Arab oil. We understand that. But are the Westerners ready to understand that it is ethically indecent for them to be the only ones to have the use of it? This war opened the way toward internationalization of responsibility and the possibility for all of us to reflect about other ways of conceiving relationships on this small planet.

Let's look at some scenarios that might create full employment in the Arab Mediterranean area and the security of women, among other things.

SCENARIO 1

Will the oil-needy Western democracies, which have emerged triumphant from the conflict, jump at the unexpected opportunity to push for the democratization of the Arab world? The economic pressure they could exert on the regimes that resist the masses' demand for democracy is enormous!

Will Western bankers and generals fly to the rescue of Arab women deprived of their rights, as they did for Kuwait? The future will tell how much sacrifice the West is prepared to make for the democracy it has taught us to love so much. The future will tell if the West will be a pioneer in establishing those universal values that it preaches and that we have come to love. The West has been given the opportunity to show us that its noble ideas really are the basis of a civilization that is more advanced, more ethical than any other. In fact, if the West uses its power to install democracy in the Arab world, it will scuttle its own interests, which the status quo, strengthened by the Gulf War, guarantees. For democracy in the Arab world means the passing of power to the millions of young people who dream of using the oil resources for their own advantage.

Will the West undermine the legitimacy of the regimes it has just saved from the storm? Will it support the demands of progressive forces and promote the creation of a civil society that would participate in decision making and demand an accounting of resources? Here lies the challenge posed by this scenario to the great Euro-American peoples, who sing of universalism and their love of democracy.

SCENARIO 2

Or will the Western states only use their influence to maintain the status quo and prop up the legitimacy of the regimes that called on them for help? The priority of buttressing their legitimacy then calls for the regimes to play the fundamentalist card. Women will again be required to wear the *hijab,* while the progressive forces have to keep quiet and pray. Relying on *taʿa* as the basis of politics will become the credo of a tele-petro-Islam transmitted by satellites. This credo will be all the knowledge that youth are entitled to as obscurantism is programmed by the electronic agenda as the modern heritage of Arab youth. The West will in great part be responsible for the avalanche of violence which will descend on all those who call for democracy, with women at the head of the list.

With globalization of the economy and globalization of responsibility, especially in the Mediterranean area, North and South are now tied to each other in fortune and misfortune. European youth are very conscious of this globalization, which looms ahead and frightens them, but which also opens extraordinary visions of solidarity, of *rahma,* of possibilities for something other than Crusades. Young people in France, Germany, and Italy are worried about what the media call the "Arab invasion." But will the maintenance of the status quo to keep up the flow of oil and petrodollars, combined with new requirements for visas for Arab travelers, solve the problem? Will the West cling to the idea of universal worth while selfishly consuming Arab oil wealth and closing its borders to Arabs? Can one trumpet universality and erect frontiers at the same time? Isn't building a Mediterranean economy based on a more equal management of oil which creates full employment and democracy everywhere the best way to stop Arab emigration to Europe? Can the West realize its ideal of one world where all can flourish together while continuing to base much of its economy on the military and space industry that it alone markets, and whose products inundate the world and especially the Arab region?

It is very laudable to want to destroy the "formidable military power" of Saddam Hussein. But this gesture is credible only if the West integrates it into a strategy of demilitarization not only of the region but of the whole planet. Destroying Saddam Hussein's nuclear capacity while restocking the arsenals of other countries in the region and investing in Western military industries is certainly not the best way to create a peaceful future.

The Arab countries devote the highest percentage of gross domestic product in the world to arms. Saudi Arabia, for example,
commits nearly one-quarter (21.8 percent) of its GDP for military
expenses. Jordan and the Democratic Republic of Yemen spend 16
percent, Syria 17 percent. By contrast, France spends 4 percent of
its GDP, the former West Germany 3.1 percent, Italy 3.2 percent,
Sweden 1.7 percent, Spain 3 percent, Canada 3.2 percent, and Japan 1 percent on weapons.[30]

How can Arab women hope to overcome opposition in their
societies and go out in search of paid work if the economies of
their countries are devoting a large part of their wealth to unpro-
ductive expenditures like the importation of weapons that don't
even serve any useful purpose, as the Gulf War amply demonstrated? If the West continues to sell arms to the Arab states,
women's chances to work out new relationships within their society will be destroyed because a society suffering from unemployment will not make any concessions to women.

One of the reasons for mounting unemployment in the Arab
countries is the debt, a problem inextricably tied to military expenditures. The editors of the *Mémento Défense-Désarmement 1989*
contend that "the net sum of the debt before 1979 could have been
20 to 30 percent lower if the borrowing Third World countries
had not bought arms. . . . Around half the arms contracts were
directly or indirectly financed by borrowing, which is characteristic of the external debt of developing countries."[31] Fundamentalism spread and flourished in the shadow of this famous debt. The
editors clearly establish the link between military expenditures and
the inflation of the debt by introducing the concept of what they
call the "opportunity cost":

The financial assets that would be available for other imports
if there had no been arms purchases are called the "opportunity cost." This concept is based on the fact that for both civil
and military imports there is only one source of financing—
exports. Rising imports require larger budgets, which at a
given moment can be covered only by exports. A government
in this case has three choices: (1) reduction in military im-

ports; (2) reduction in commercial imports; or (3) increase in foreign currency provided by loans. Experience shows that it is above all the last option that was chosen.[32]

The military option is contrary to the interests of Arab citizens in general, and to those of women in particular. No leftist movement in the Arab world can offer a serious alternative if it doesn't make the demilitarization of the region a priority. Arab women too must mobilize around the issue of demilitarization; otherwise any hope for an improvement in their lot is vain. The only way for the Arab nations is that of Japan, which allocates just 1 percent of its budget for defense, neither more nor less. Who will be the loser in this business? The weapons factories in the West, and some middlemen. That's all. Who will be the winner? The whole world, headed by the citizens of the Western countries. For the West to focus on producing something other than weapons would be the best proof of its concern for implementing universal values.

While waiting, we can dream with Julia Kristeva about a future in which the *gharib,* "the strange" and "the stranger," will no longer be frightening: can "the stranger," who was "the enemy" in primitive societies, disappear in the modern world?[33]

I am an incurable optimist. There are now unprecedented opportunities for creating a better world. In Third World societies millions of people like me, who belong to groups that only recently were excluded from knowledge, have had access to that manna from heaven since the Second World War. We must not fall into the victim mentality and moan about what a miserable century this is. It is a fabulous century, at least for the countries of the Third World, which used to stagnate in material, political, and cultural deprivation. In countries like mine, many of our doctors and brilliant professors began life as shepherds, and they often recall this fact with a certain pride, especially to communicate to their students a sense of the wonder felt by all those in the Third World who have had access to an unhoped-for education. Let us have fewer weapons and more learning. Then we will have a world that I would love to travel around, a world in whose creation I would be proud to participate. I know there are untold millions of others who want such a world.

170

Farid al-din Attar, my favorite of the Sufis, dreamed nine centuries ago of a marvelous planet inhabited by fabulous birds that were much like us—who wanted to find themselves, who wanted to travel, but were afraid. Their desire for knowledge, however, was so strong that it transformed their lives. Attar sang of that Sufi Islam that is totally unknown to the Western media. It will probably be the only successful challenger to the electronic agenda, for it offers something the latter can never threaten nor replace: the spirituality that gives wings, opening you up to the other like a flower. A flower is not frightened by a *gharib*. A *gharib* might be a Simorgh! And each of us has a Simorgh within us.

Conclusion
The Simorgh Is Us!

It happened in Nishapur in Iran in the spring of A.D. 1175. A man dreamed of a world without fear, without boudnaries, where you could travel very far and find yourself in the company of strangers whom you knew as you knew yourself, strangers who were neither hostile nor aggressive. It was the land of the Simorgh.

In his long meditations in Nishapur, all by himself Attar imagined that land where strangeness only enriched what we are to the ultimate degree. He committed his dream to paper, a long poem that he called *Mantiq al-tayr* (The Conference of the Birds). It instantly became famous, but intolerance and violence knocked one night at Attar's door. Genghis Khan's Mongol soldiers murdered Attar in 1230. The poet died, but the dream lived on through the centuries and continues to haunt our imaginations.

Thousands of birds had heard of a fabulous being called the Simorgh, whom they longed to see and know. They decided to go together, by their thousands, to the place where they were told he could be found. For years and years they crossed rivers and oceans to find the Simorgh, that fabulous creature, radiant and dazzling. Many birds died along the way and never finished the journey. Fatigue and the rigors of the climate decimated most of the seekers. Only thirty succeeded in arriving at the gates of the fortress of the legendary Simorgh. But when they were finally received, a surprise

172

awaited them which we will understand better if we know that in Persian *si* means thirty and *morgh* means birds:

There in the Simorgh's radiant face they saw
Themselves, the Simorgh of the world—with awe
They gazed, and dared at last to comprehend
They were the Simorgh and the journey's end.
They see the Simorgh—at themselves they stare,
And see a second Simorgh standing there;
They look at both and see the two are one,
That this is that, that this, the goal is won.
They ask (but inwardly; they make no sound)
The meaning of these mysteries that confound
Their puzzled ignorance. . . . [1]

When the thirty birds, dazzled and baffled, asked the Simorgh to explain this strange reality to them, he talked to them of a mirror that could reflect the whole planet, with all its differences and its individualities. They asked him to reveal the great secret, to explain the mystery of why " 'we' is not distinguished here from 'you'?"[2] The Simorgh explained to them what is still not understood eight centuries later by our leaders: that the community, indeed the whole world, can be a mirror of individualities, and that its strength will then only be greater:

"I am a mirror set before your eyes,
And all who come before my splendour see
Themselves, their own unique reality;
You came as thirty birds and therefore saw
These selfsame thirty birds, not less nor more;
If you had come as forty, fifty—here
An answering forty, fifty would appear; . . .
And since you came as thirty birds, you see
These thirty birds when you discover Me,
The Simorgh, Truth's last flawless jewel, the light
In which you will be lost to mortal sight,
Dispersed to nothingness until once more
You find in Me the selves you were before."[3]

173

Conclusion

Since that time, the Simorgh, banned in the Orient of the palaces, has haunted women's tales and children's dreams. Today the cry for pluralism no longer has to hide behind metaphysical allegories. We can bring a new world into being through all the scientific advances that allow us to communicate, to engage in unlimited dialogue, to create that global mirror in which all cultures can shine in their uniqueness. Nothing makes me more exuberant than the vision of this new world, and the fact that we must go forward toward it without any barriers no longer frightens me. How are we to learn to stride into the abyss and be like the wind? How are we to be defenseless like the forest? How can we have uncertainty as our country? It is surely the poets who will be our guides among these new galaxies.

Notes

INTRODUCTION
THE GULF WAR: FEAR AND ITS BOUNDARIES

1. On the concept of the *hijab* and especially its visual, spatial, and ethical aspects see my *The Veil and the Male Elite: A Feminist Interpretation of Women's Rights in Islam* (Reading, Mass.: Addison-Wesley, 1991), pp. 93–97. The British edition is entitled *Women and Islam: An Historical and Theological Enquiry* (Oxford: Blackwell, 1991).
2. The Suq al-Sabat is supplied with rejects from factories that make shoes for export. The narrowness of the street makes it an excellent place for communication. During times of important political events, all the radios and television sets are turned on, and buying and selling come to a stop when the news is being broadcast. Thanks to their friendship with the factory workers in Casablanca, 'Ali and his neighbors in the street can order custom-fit shoes for the shopper, with a choice of colors and features. Parallel to the mainstream shoe industry, the informal network between workers and small storeowners attracts a growing clientele, especially of fashion-conscious young people.
3. In dates cited in this style the first date or dates are the years according to the Muslim calendar, the second the years according to the Christian calendar.
4. For the meaning of *'awra* see Tabari, *Tafsir* (Beirut: Dar al-Fikr, 1984), vol. 21, p. 136.
5. See the proverbial *tabarruj* of the *jahiliyya* in sura 33, v. 33, and the commentary in Tabari, *Tafsir,* vol. 21, pp. 3ff. See also sura 24, v. 60 (and Tabari's commentary in vol. 18, p. 165), where it is stated that a woman past menopause, who no longer has hopes of marriage or childbearing, may take off her veils.
6. On the concept of *muhsanat* (protected women) see sura 4, v. 24–25, and Tabari, *Tafsir,* vol. 5, pp. 1ff.

175

Notes

7. All quotations from the Koran are from the English translation by Marmaduke Pickthall, *The Meaning of the Glorious Koran* (New York: Dorset, n.d.).

CHAPTER 1 FEAR OF THE FOREIGN WEST

1. Here I am indebted to ʿAbd al-Fattah Kilitu, who was the first to analyze systematically the link between the West and strangeness; see his *Al-adab wa al-gharaba* (Literature and Strangeness) (Beirut: Dar al-Taliʿa, 1982).

2. *The Book of the Thousand Nights and a Night,* trans. Richard F. Burton (N.p.: Privately printed by the Burton Club, n.d.), vol. 4, pp. 130–31.

3. Ibid., pp. 131–32.

4. I must clarify why it is that I often use the words "Arab" and "Islam" interchangeably, and why from here on I focus on Arabs and the Arabic language. It is certainly not because the other cultures that contributed to this extraordinary mosaic that is Islam are minor. I am in a poor position to discuss Pan-Arabism because, like the majority of Moroccans, I am ethnically rather Berber. This small detail posed a problem at the time of the formation of the Arab League. If it is Arab, what are Berbers and Sudanese doing in it? The Moroccan leader Allal al-Fasi explains in the last pages of his book *Al-haraka al-istiqlaliyya fi al-maghrib al-ʿarabi* (The Independence Movements in the Arab Maghrib) (Cairo: Matabaʿat al-Risala, 1948) that one of the clauses of the league's charter stipulates that the countries of the Maghrib are an integral part of the Arab world, which is above all else a culture. I thus do not distinguish between the words "Arab" and "Muslim"—not that the two words overlap, because there are Muslims who are not Arabs (Iranians, Turks, Chinese, etc.) and Arabs who are not Muslims (Arab Christian or Jewish minorities in the Middle East), but because Islam was originally expressed in the Arabic language. Although other languages and cultures have modulated the regional cultural expression of Islam, the fact remains that the importance of Arabic as the original language of the sacred overrides all differences. So if in this book I examine the Arab Islamic culture only through the Arabic language, the schemas and concepts that emerge may help us decipher all the cultures of the Islamic tradition, even those whose language is not Arabic. I am not saying that Islam can be reduced to Arabism, which would be both racist and absurd, and in any case would not help us see things more clearly. I am simply stating that by exploring the nuances of the Arabic words that express Islam, we can understand certain fundamental schemas of that culture. I therefore limit myself to examining the way of thinking and seeing of the group to which I belong, the group that is part of both Arab and Muslim culture. I say "culture" and not "race" because many Algerians and Moroccans as well as Sudanese are not ethnically Arab but are immersed in the Arabic language and Muslim culture, and the two are intimately linked. What I am trying to do is explore what I call our mental territory, the stock of

176

images and symbols that generate our emotions and thoughts, our cultural schemas, the landmarks of our civilization—all of which allow us not only to understand the world but to situate ourselves in it and act in it. It is in this context that Islam and language become practically one and the same thing.

5. Imam al-Qurtubi, *Al-intiqa' fi fada'il al-tal'at al-'a'imma al-fuqaha, malik, shafi'i wa abu hanifa* (Beirut: Dar al-'Ilmiyya, n.d.), p. 44. The author died in year 463 of the Hejira.

6. Ibn Khallikan, *Wafayat al-a'yan* (Beirut: Dar Sadir, n.d.), vol. 2, p. 140. Ibn Khallikan died in year 681 of the Hejira. Those who wish to know more about Hallaj should read what Massignon has written, especially *La passion de Hallaj, martyre mystique de l'Islam,* 4 vols. (Paris: Gallimard, 1975).

CHAPTER 2 FEAR OF THE IMAM

1. See Fatima Mernissi, *The Forgotten Queens of Islam* (Cambridge: Polity Press, forthcoming 1993), chap. 2.

2. Bernard Lewis, "Islam et société civile," in *Islam et politique en Proche Orient aujourd'hui* (Paris: Gallimard, 1991), p. 29.

3. Shahrastani, *Al-milal wa al-nihal* (Beirut: Dar Sa'b, 1986), vol. 1, p. 114. The author died in year 547 of the Hejira.

4. Al-Mas'udi, *Muruj al-dhahab* (Beirut: Dar al-Ma'rifa, 1982), vol. 2, p. 423. Al-Mas'udi died in year 346 of the Hejira (A.D. 956).

5. Shahrastani, *Al-milal wa al-nihal,* vol. 1, p. 115. Concerning the use of modern fundamentalist slogans, see Qadi 'Ashmawi, *Al-Islam al-siyasi* (Political Islam) (Algiers: Mawfim li-Nashr, 1990), chap. 1, "Hakimiyyat Allah, nahj al-tughat" (The Power of God or the Way of the Despots). The French translation, entitled *L'Islamisme contre l'Islam,* is published by Editions la Découverte (1989).

6. Shahrastani, *Al-milal wa al-nihal,* vol. 1, p. 122.

7. 'Ashmawi, *Al-Islam al siyasi,* pp. 23ff. 'Ashmawi, who defends representative democracy against rebel democracy, gives a very concise analysis of this point.

8. Ibn Hazm, *Al-Rasa'il* (Beirut: Al-Mu'assasa al-'Arabiyya li Dirasat wa Nashr, 1981), vol. 2, pp. 106ff. Ibn Hazm died in year 456 of the Hejira (the eleventh century).

9. After 'Uthman there was only one more orthodox caliph, 'Ali, whose successor, by violating the rule of accession to the caliphate, was considered outside orthodoxy. The caliphate was made hereditary, which is regarded as contrary to the spirit of Islam, instituting despotism with the first dynasty, the Umayyads, in 31/661.

10. Ibn Hazm, *Al-Rasa'il,* vol. 2, p. 102.

11. Ibid., p. 103.

12. Shajarat al-Durr was one of those who used the *hammam* as the site for revenge on her husband, ʿIzz al-Din Aybak, the sovereign of Mamluk Egypt; see Mernissi, *Forgotten Sultanas,* chap. 6.
13. Al-Masʿudi, *Muruj,* vol. 4, p. 20.
14. Ibid.
15. *Lisan al-ʿArab,* entry for *shariʿa.*
16. Abu Zahra, *Al-madahi al-islamiyya* (Cairo: Maktabat al-Adab, n.d.), pp. 5–6.
17. Shahrastani, *Al-milal wa al-nihal,* p. 45.
18. Al-Masʿudi, *Muruj,* vol. 3, p. 236.
19. For a concise discussion and a list of references see the article "Muʿtazila," in *Encyclopedia of Islam.*
20. Marshall G. S. Hodgson, *The Venture of Islam: Conscience and History in a World Civilization* (Chicago: University of Chicago Press, 1974), vol. 1, pp. 410ff.
21. See the special issue of *Muslim World* devoted to fundamentalism (January 1990).
22. Muhammad ʿAbid al-Jabiri, *Nahnu wa al-tharwa* (Beirut: Al-Markaz al-Thaqafi al-ʿArabi, Dar al-Baida, and Dar al-Taliʿa, 1980).
23. Muhammad ʿAbid al-Jabiri, *Taqwin al-ʿaql al-ʿarabi* (Beirut: Dar al-Taliʿa, 1980).
24. Sharastani, *Al-milal wa al-nihal,* vol. 1, p. 37.

CHAPTER 3 FEAR OF DEMOCRACY

1. *La semaine internationale* (a weekly review of United Nations activities), FI-37-87, February 9, 1987, p. 7.
2. *World Military Expenditures and Arms Transfers* (Washington, D.C.: U.S. Arms and Disarmament Agency, 1984), pp. 8–9.
3. Ibid.
4. Scott Armstrong, "Eye of the Storm," *Mother Jones,* November/December 1991, p. 34.
5. James Davison Hunter, "On Secular Humanism," *Dialogue* (U.S. Information Agency, Washington, D.C.), February 1991, p. 70.
6. Ibid., p. 66.
7. Hichem Djait, "Culture et politique dans le monde Arabe," *Le Debat,* "Islam et politique" (special issue), 1991, p. 71.
8. Hunter, "On Secular Humanism," p. 70.
9. F. Jaʿdan, "Usul al-taqaddum ʿind mufakkir al-Islam," quoted in Djait, "Culture et politique," p. 37.
10. ʿAli Umlil, *Al-tasamuh hasab al-islahiyya al-islamiyya* (Beirut: Dar al-Thanawbar, 1985); published in French as *Islam et état national* (Casablanca: Editions le Fennec, 1991).
11. Ibid., p. 47.

12. Anwar al-Jundi, *Muhakamat fikr Taha Husayn* (Cairo: Dar al-I'sam, 1984), p. 15.

13. I don't recall exactly whether these childhood readings were chosen by the teacher from Taha Husayn's *Hadith al-arbi'a* or his *'Ala hamish al-sira;* probably they were from both books. A rereading of the two works last year reintroduced to my rather limited cultural life in Rabat the luminosity of those happy mornings at school in Fez, although I didn't find the exact pages that produced the magic I had experienced in my first acquaintance with them.

14. Rifa'at al-Tahtawi, "Al-a'mal al-kamila," quoted in Umlil, *Al-tasamuh hasab,* p. 117.

15. My first education, which I describe in Chapter 5, was in a Koranic school. I was enrolled in first grade in a nationalist school, and I did my secondary school studies in a "collège for young Muslim ladies," an institution financed by the French protectorate (that is, by our taxes). To tell the truth, moving from one institution to another had no bad effect on me. Perhaps it was because the spirit of Descartes and Enlightenment philosophy, reflected through the mirror of a French colonial lycée and taught by Catholic teachers, didn't succeed in shining through. In any case, no one ever taught me tolerance, and I never saw it practiced during my long period of schooling. I learned it not from my teachers but in chance encounters with humble people in the shops, alleys, and neglected areas of the Fez medina.

16. See Saad Eddin Ibrahim, "Anatomy of Egypt's Militant Islamic Groups," *International Journal of Middle East Studies* 12 (1980), pp. 423–53.

17. See the excellent studies done for UNESCO by a group of Arab experts: Ramdane Ouahes, *La science et la technologie dans les états Arabes à l'horizon 2000* (May 1988); and F. Mardam Bey and L. Soliman, *La culture dans le monde Arabe* (July 1988).

18. Djait, "Culture et politique," p. 88.

19. I am talking about the countries of Western Europe. I am not well acquainted with Eastern Europe; I do not know the languages, and my strolls in the streets of Prague and Berlin in September 1991 were too brief for me to make anything but a superficial judgment. I did begin to sense in East Berlin and in Prague something resembling the Arab feeling of *'azma,* the feeling of malaise and self-deprecation. Some little details—the weary, disillusioned comments of taxi drivers in Prague and East Berlin, for example—had a familiar ring. But it could be that I was wrong. It would be interesting to conduct a public opinion poll to measure the feelings of discontent with the economy in both Eastern Europe and the Arab world, and then compare the findings to learn how the crippling of the democratic heritage is experienced there and here.

20. The quotation is from sura 2, v. 186.

21. On workers' feelings about their rights as employees, see Fatima Mernissi, *Chahrazad n'est pas Marocaine,* 2nd ed. (Casablanca: Editions le Fennec, 1991), p. 85. See also the interviews with workers in the new edition of idem, *Le*

Notes

Maroc raconté par ses femmes, which is entitled *Le monde n'est pas un harem* (Paris: Albin Michel, 1991).

CHAPTER 4 THE UNITED NATIONS CHARTER

1. *Multilateral Treaties Deposited with the Secretary-General as of December 31, 1987* (New York: United Nations, 1988), pp. 162–63.
2. See *Human Rights: Status of International Instruments* (New York: United Nations, 1987).
3. See Nouredine Saadi, *Femmes et loi en Algérie* (Casablanca: Editions le Fennec, 1991); Chérif Chamari Alya, *Femmes et loi en Tunisie* (Casablanca: Editions le Fennec, 1991); Abderrazak Moulay Rachid, *Femmes et loi au Maroc* (Casablanca: Editions le Fennec, 1991).
4. All figures on radio and television programs are taken from the *UNESCO Statistical Yearbook* for 1985 and 1987.
5. See, for example, *Amnesty International Report,* 1989.
6. It is always wonderful to run into Arab intellectuals in Paris and London and to be able to buy their banned books there.
7. See, for example, the brochures of the Arab Human Rights Organization, which are beginning to circulate in Cairo and the whole Arab world. Published during the 1980s, they include results of various human rights investigations and translations of basic United Nations documents.
8. On the occasion of the publication of his book *Le onzième commandement,* Glucksmann remarked: "Although Muslim fundamentalism is contained today (not without crises, Kuwait-style) by a dissuasive equilibrium, it can be destroyed only from within by the Muslim peoples themselves. It is up to them to understand that it is not a question of smashing that provocative Western window that is Israel, but rather of their assenting to the comfort, and so to the difficulties, of a modern state"; interview in *L'Express,* September 19, 1991, p. 118.
9. For information on the occurrences of words in the Koran I rely mainly on Muhammad Fuad 'Abd al-Baqi, *Al-mu'jam al-mufahras li alfaz al-qur'an al-karim* (Beirut: Dar al-Fikr, 1981).

CHAPTER 5 THE KORAN

1. Imam Ibn Kathir, *Tafsir al-qur'an al-'azim* (Beirut: Dar al-Ma'rifa, 1987), vol. 1, p. 8.
2. The standard reference is Ibn Hisham, *Al-sira al-nabawiyya* (Beirut: Dar Ihya' al-Tharwa al-'Arabi, n.d.). Ibn Hisham died in year 216 of the Hejira. Personally I prefer the *sira* (biography) of Ibn Sa'd, who was born 167 years after the Prophet and whose work is extraordinarily subtle in its details: Ibn Sa'd, *Al-*

tabaqat al-kubra (Beirut: Dar al-Fakr, 1985). Other historians reproduce more or less verbatim the account of Ibn Hisham.

3. Ibn Hisham, *Sira;* Ibn Saʿd, *Tabaqat;* al-Masʿudi, *Muruj,* vol. 2, p. 282.

4. There are differing opinions about the length of the period of revelation; some say twenty years, others twenty-three, and still others twenty-five. On this subject see Jalal al-Din al-Suyuti, *Asrar tartib al-qurʾan* (N.p.: Dar al-Iʿtisam, 1978, pp. 26ff; Abi al-Hasan ʿAli al-Nisaburi, *Asbab al-nuzul* (Beirut: Dar al-Kutub al-ʿIlmiya, 1986), p. 2. Al-Suyuti died in year 911 of the Hejira (the sixteenth century), al-Nisaburi in year 468 (the eleventh century).

5. Al-Nisaburi, *Asbab al-nuzul,* p. 7.

6. Tabari, *Tafsir jamiʿ al-bayan ʿan taʾwil ayi al-qurʾan* (Cairo: Dar al-Maʿarif, n.d.), vol. 2, p. 254.

7. Al-Suyuti, *Asrar,* p. 71.

8. Ibn Kathir, *Tafsir al-qurʾan,* vol. 1, p. 8.

9. Ibn Saʿd, *Tabaqat,* vol. 2, pp. 355ff.

10. Introduction to al-Suyuti, *Asrar,* p. 44.

11. Shahrastani, *Al-milal wa al-nihal,* vol. 1, pp. 128ff.

12. Ibid., pp. 114ff.

13. One of the most recent and most pertinent analyses of the education of children as the key factor in determining class structure in Morocco is Aicha Belarbi, *Enfance au quotidien* (Casablanca: Editions le Fennec, 1991).

14. Philippe Aziz, "Les financiers de l'Islam," *Le Point,* May 27–June 2, 1991, p. 21.

CHAPTER 6 FEAR OF FREEDOM OF THOUGHT

1. *Lisan al-ʿArab,* entry for the root *s-l-m.*

2. Ibn Saʿd, *Tabaqat,* vol. 2, p. 136.

3. Ibn al-Kalbi, *Kitab al-asnam* (Book of Idols) (Cairo: Matbaʿat Dar al-Kutub al-Misriyya, 1924), p. 33.

4. ʿAbd al-Baqi, *Al-muʿjam,* p. 379.

5. Tabari, *Tafsir,* vol. 7, p. 208; *Lisan al-ʿArab.*

6. *Lisan al-ʿArab.*

7. Tabari, *Tafsir,* vol. 7, p. 208.

8. *ʿAql* (reason) in this sense has a strict meaning, that of identifying with the group's laws. *ʿAql,* "reasonable behavior," is the capacity of the individual to restrict behavior and curb individual desire, *hawa,* in accordance with the rules of the *umma.* In this context, *ʿaql* as the group's laws is in complete conflict with the concept of reason as personal opinion in the meaning of *muʿtazila.* A Muslim author has devoted an entire book to this fundamental conflict in Islam between *hawa* and *ʿaql;* see Fatna A. Sabbah, *Woman in the Muslim Unconscious* (New York: Pergamon, 1984).

9. ʿAbd al-Baqi, *Al-muʿjam.*

10. F. Rosenthal, the article "Hurriyya," in *Encyclopedia of Islam,* 2nd ed. I do not agree with Rosenthal about the Sufis. Submission was part of their doctrine, but there was also glorification of the individual as the seat of the divine. It is a point of view that many contemporary authors are advancing, especially those who translate Arabic into a Western language. Notable among them is the Tunisian Abdelwahed Meddeb, whose magnificent voice can be heard in French behind those of the Sufis he has presented to us.

11. The *shawush* holds one of the most fascinating offices of modern Moroccan bureaucracy. In principle he is a sort of concierge for a government minister. In fact he is one of the most powerful men in the Moroccan government because although ministers change, he remains, and he knows everything that goes on, both official and confidential.

12. I am talking about the city of Fez in northern Morocco. When I was studying at the Université Mohammed V in Rabat in the 1960s, boys from other parts of the country would tease me by asking if I came from the city of donkeys. The people of Fez, who are decried for their arrogance, are often insulted as being from city where donkeys are the majority of the population. It wasn't until I was forty years old that I managed to control my anger at this.

13. Al-Bukhari, *Al-Sahih* (Beirut: Dar al-Maʿrifa, 1978), vol. 4, p. 44.

14. Ibn al-Kalbi, *Kitab al-asnam,* p. 8.

15. *Lisan al-ʿArab,* entries for the roots *k-l-q, b-d-ʿ*.

16. Ibid., entry for *zindiq*.

17. Ibn Kathir, *Tafsir al-qurʾan,* vol. 1, p. 49.

18. Tabari, *Tafsir,* vol. 23, p. 125.

19. Ibn al-Kalbi, *Kitab al-asnam,* p. 53.

20. Toufiq Fahd, *Le panthéon de l'Arabie Centrale à la veille de l'hégire* (Paris: Geuthner, 1968), p. 29.

21. Tabari, *Tafsir,* vol. 23, p. 127.

22. Ibid.

23. *Lisan al-ʿArab,* entries for *hizb, shiʿa*. See also Mernissi, *The Forgotten Queens of Islam,* chap. 7.

24. Is this one of the reasons that even after thirty years' residence, North African immigrants in Europe still talk about "returning"? We shouldn't assign too much importance to the influence of sacred symbology, but a triumphant return "back home" remains a strong idea in the collective unconscious. Only rarely can one accept being defeated for good, making it necessary to seek one's fortune by putting down roots elsewhere.

CHAPTER 7 FEAR OF INDIVIDUALISM

1. Ibn Hisham, *Sira,* vol. 1, p. 83.

2. Ibn al-Kalbi, *Kitab al-asnam,* p. 28. Ibn Hisham recounts the same incident in his *Sira,* but there the famous person involved was unnamed. He does none-theless mention that some historians attribute the anecdote to Imruʿu al-Qais.

3. A Koranic example in which Pharaoh is described as acting arrogantly toward Moses and refusing to obey because he takes himself for a god—behavior that results in punishment—is in sura 79, v. 15–26:

> 15. Hath there come unto thee the history of Moses?
> 16. How his Lord called him in the holy vale of Tuwa,
> 17. (Saying:) Go thou unto Pharaoh—Lo! he hath rebelled—
> 18. And say (unto him): Hast thou (will) to grow (in grace)?
> 19. Then I will guide thee to thy Lord and thou shalt fear (Him).
> 20. And he showed him the tremendous token.
> 21. But he denied and disobeyed,
> 22. Then turned he away in haste,
> 23. Then gathered he and summoned
> 24. And proclaimed: "I (Pharaoh) am your Lord the Highest."
> 25. So Allah seized him (and made him) an example for the after (life) and for the former.
> 26. Lo! herein is indeed a lesson for him who feareth.

4. See Mernissi, *The Forgotten Queens of Islam,* chap. 9.

5. Khayr al-Din al-Zarkali, *Al-aʿlam, qamus ashʿar al-rijal wa al-nisaʾ min al-ʿarab wa al-mustaʿrabin wa al-mustashraqin* (Beirut: Dar al-ʿIlm li al-Malayin, 1983).

6. Al-Masʿudi, *Muruj,* vol. 4, p. 18. Al-Maʾmun's references to Moses' throwing down his staff and to his burning hand are from sura 28, vv. 31–32.

7. Al-Jahiz, *Kitab al-hayawan* (Book of Animals), quoted in Ibn Kalbi, *Kitab al-asnam,* p. 34.

8. Ibn Hisham, *Sira,* vol. 4, p. 53.

9. Hodgson, *The Venture of Islam,* vol. 2, p. 543.

10. Dariyus Shayegané, "La Déchirure," *Le Debat,* reprinted in "Islam et poli-tique" (special issue), 1991, p. 296. In his book *Le regard mutilé* (Paris: Albin Michel, 1989), Shayegané gives a sophisticated analysis of the Iranian situa-tion and of what happens in a Muslim society when the normal course of modernizing is crudely blocked, freezing enthusiasm and destroying hopes.

11. In *The Veil and the Male Elite* I explained that in the course of its egalitarian revolution Islam allowed women to emerge as subjects, whereas in the *jahiliyya* they had had the status of objects, inherited and passed on like live-stock. At the rise of Islam women were among the Companions of the Prophet and as such participated actively in community affairs, claiming their rights and sometimes succeeding in obtaining them. With the advent of the Umayyad despotism, however, women sank back into a slavelike status like that which they had had in the *jahiliyya.* This theory is apparently disputed,

because the book was banned in Morocco several months after its publication in French (Paris: Albin Michel, 1987).

CHAPTER 8 FEAR OF THE PAST

1. Al-Jahiz, "Kitab al-hijab," in *Rasaʿil al-Jahiz* (Cairo: Maktabat al-Khanji, 1968), vol. 2, pp. 25–86; *Kitab al-taj fi akhlaq al-muluk* (Beirut: Al-Sharika al-Lubnaniyya li al-Kitab, n.d.). In *Kitab al-taj* al-Jahiz presents a lengthy discussion of the use of the caliph's *hijab,* including the occasions on which it was used in daily life to hide the caliph from his entourage. An excellent French translation by Charles Pellat is available, entitled *Le Livre de la couronne* (Paris: Société d'Edition Les Belles Lettres, 1954).

2. Despite the veil thrown across the degraded past, characterized as a "time of ignorance," the Arabs have always been very interested in the pre-Islamic cults, and all the early writers on religious history devoted pages and pages to it. I will list a few that I like most: Ibn Hisham, *Sira;* Ibn Habib, *Kitab al-mukhabbar;* Ibn al-Kalbi, *Kitab al-asnam* (English), trans. N. A. Faris (Princeton: Princeton University Press, 1952); Tabari, *Tafsir;* Ibn Saʿd, *Tabaqat;* Yaqut, *Muʿjam al-buldan* (often quoted, but I have not read it); al-Masʿudi, *Muruj.*

   Interest in the *jahiliyya* and its beliefs has not lessened with the years; modern writers carry on this tradition, especially those who explore pre-Islamic poetry: Taha Husayn, *Fi al-shiʿr al-jahili* (1926); idem, *Fi al-adab al-jahili* (1927); Ahmad al-ʿUla, *Muhadarat fi tarikh al-ʿarab* (Baghdad: Maktabat al-Muthanna, 1960), vol. 1, "Al-din al-jahili"; and Ahmad al-Hufi, *Al-marʾa fi al-shiʿr al-jahili* (Woman in Pre-Islamic Poetry) (Cairo: Dar al-Nahda, n.d.).

3. Ibn Hisham, *Sira,* vol. 1, pp. 86–87.

4. Ibn al-Kalbi, *Kitab al-asnam,* pp. 13–14.

5. Toufiq Fahd, *Le panthéon de l'Arabie Centrale,* p. 125.

6. Ibid., p. 126.

7. Ibn al-Kalbi, *Kitab al-asnam,* p. 15.

8. Ibid., p. 16.

9. Dominique Sourdel, *Les cultes du Hauran à l'epoque Romaine* (Paris: Geuthner, 1952), p. 69.

10. Ibid., pp. 73 (esp. nn. 2 and 3), 74.

11. Ibn al-Kalbi, *Kitab al-asnam,* p. 15.

12. Toufic Fahd, *Le panthéon de l'Arabie Centrale,* p. 40.

13. Al-ʿUla, *Muhadarat,* p. 182; Toufic Fahd, *Le panthéon de l'Arabie Centrale,* p. 169.

14. Tabari, *Tafsir,* vol. 8, p. 43.

15. Ibid., vol. 8, p. 51.

16. Ibn Hisham, *Sira,* vol. 1, pp. 160ff.

17. Toufic Fahd, *Le panthéon de l'Arabie Centrale,* p. 168.

18. Al-Masʿudi, *Muruj,* vol. 2, p. 231.

19. Ibid., p. 248.

20. On this subject see Y. Moubarac, "Les études d'épigraphie Sud-Sémitique et la naissance de l'Islam," *Revue des études Islamiques* (1955 and 1957). On Venus in particular see Franz Cumont, "Le culte de Venus chez les Arabes au Ier siècle," *Syria* 8 (1927), p. 368; idem, *Monuments des mystères de Miothra,* vol. 1, p. 231; Fr. Lenormant, *Sur le culte paien de la Kaabah;* Jacqueline Pirenne, "La déesse des reliefs Sabéens," *Syria* 42 (1965); idem, "Stele de la déesse Dhat Himyam," *Syria* 37 (1960). In the latter article see particularly p. 343: "The papyrus Oxy. 13, from the first century of our era . . . has preserved for us the great litany of Isis. And it identifies her for us as Astarte in Phoenicia, Atargatis in Hierapolis, as Anaitis in Persia, and attests that she is also 'a great goddess in Arabia.' We know that Isis, likened to the planet Venus Anaitis in Persia, was both Ishtar and Venus; the Phoenician Astarte is obviously Venus."

21. Tabari, *Tafsir,* vol. 24, pp. 121, 21.

22. Yaqut, *Mu'jam al-buldan,* quoted by Toufic Fahd in *Le panthéon de l'Arabie Centrale,* pp. 150ff.

23. Tabari, *Tafsir,* vol. 27, p. 88.

24. Ibn Habib, *Kitab al-mukhabbar,* p. 157.

25. Numerous verses in the Koran deal with the incredulity toward the idea of resurrection, indicating the amount of effort the Prophet had to put into the psychological transformation of the Arabs. Among the many references are sura 22, v. 5; sura 11, v. 7; sura 17, v. 98; sura 23, v. 37; and sura 34, v. 16.

CHAPTER 9 FEAR OF THE PRESENT

1. Hodgson, *The Venture of Islam,* vol. 2, p. 168.

2. Ouahes, *Science et technologie,* p. 49.

3. Al-Hakim, the sovereign of the Fatimid dynasty who reigned in Egypt (386–411/996–1020), was at first mad about astrology and then just plain mad, plunging Cairo into a bloodbath by irrationally ordering the execution of innocents. The reason for his madness is not known. We do know, however, that he would often leave his palace at night to contemplate the stars on a forested hill near Cairo. Astrology played an important role in ritual and decision making for al-Hakim, in accordance with the central place of the stars in the Shi'ite vision of the world. At barely thirty years old he sank into madness, which began with his fascination with the stars, the flight of time that inscribes the approach of death in the heavens, in the succession of days and nights.

The caliph al-Hakim is one of the most extraordinary figures in Muslim history. I came on him for the first time when I was doing research for my book *The Forgotten Queens of Islam,* in which I devote a chapter to him (chap. 9, "The Lady of Cairo," q.v.). During our education we Sunni Muslims receive little information about Shi'ite Islam, and the importance of the stars and time in the Shi'ite vision of Islam surprised and captivated me. Another Moroccan seems to have fallen under the spell of the monstrous yet very human al-Hakim: the brilliant philosopher Bensalem Himmich, who after ten years of research wrote a fictional account of his life, *Majnun al-hukm* (London: Riad el-Rais Books, 1991).

4. The answers to the inexorable encroachment of death offered by Western technology have been essentially cosmetic—youth creams, tonics, and the like. One can imagine the terrible crisis the world's religions would face if an elixir of immortality were found. While we wait, however, the religions fare better than science on this terrain, for they alone offer assurance of a second life after death—not a negligible point, especially if one's earthly life was rather mediocre.

5. Bertrand Russell, *Religion and Science* (London: Oxford University Press, 1956), p. 19.

6. Ibid., p. 24.

7. Read any issue of *Intersignes,* but especially that entitled "Entre psychanalyse et Islam" (Spring 1990).

8. On the concept of *ishraq* see, for example, the chapter "Sohravardi et la philosophie de la lumière," in Henri Corbin, *Histoire de la philosophie Islamique* (Paris: Gallimard, 1986), pp. 285ff.

9. Tabari, *Tarikh al-umam wa al-muluk* (Beirut: Dar al-Fikr, 1979), vol. 3, p. 90.

10. Ibid., vol. 2, p. 252.

11. Ibid., vol. 1, p. 252.

12. Ibid.

13. Ibid.

14. Ibid., vol. 2, pp. 253, 254.

15. Ibid., p. 254.

16. Tabari, *Tafsir,* vol. 10, pp. 129ff.

17. Al-Mas'udi, *Muruj,* vol. 2, p. 203.

18. *The New Encyclopedia Britannica 1991,* vol. 3, p. 606.

19. Jacques Attali, *Histoire du temps* (Paris: Fayard, 1982), p. 286.

20. Ibid., p. 284.

21. Opuahes, *Science et technologie.*

22. For the failure of Arabsat see the very technical report of Hassane Till, *La communication audiovisuelle dans le Monde Arabe* (UNESCO, July 1988). See also Barrak Anissa, "Arabsat: bilan et perspectives," Mémoire de DEA en Sciences de l'information, Université Paris 2 (February 1986).

23. Attali, *Histoire du temps,* p. 62.

24. Joseph Campbell, *Myths to Live By* (New York: Bantam Books, 1972), p. 242.

25. Ibid., p. 244.

26. Alvin Toffler, *Power Shift: Knowledge, Wealth, and Violence at the Edge of the 21st Century* (New York: Bantam Books, 1990), p. 20.

Notes

1. Muhammad al-Fasi, *Chants anciens des femmes de Fes* (pirated edition published in Morocco, n.d.), p. 38, quatrain 43. The original in Arabic is entitled *Rubayat nisa' Fas* (Casablanca: Dar Qurtuba, 1986). The author reports that the original French version was published in Paris in 1967.

2. Adonis, *Chants de Mihyar le Damascène,* trans. Anne Wade Minkowski (Paris: Sindbad, 1983). The original in Arabic was entitled *Aghani Mihyar al-Dimashqi* (Beirut: Dar al-Adab, 1988).

3. Muhammad ʿAbd al-Hakim al-Qadi, *Al-libas wa al-zina: al-sunna al-mutahhara* (Cairo: Dar al-Hadith, 1988).

4. Al-Maqrizi, *Al-Khitat* (Cairo: Maktabat al-Thaqafa al-Diniyya, 1987). Al-Maqrizi died in year 845 of the Hejira.

5. Abi al-Falah ʿAbd al-Hayy Ibn al-ʿImad al-Hanbali, *Shazarat al-dhahab fi akhbar man dhahab* (Beirut: Manshurat Dar al-Afaq al-Jadida, n.d.), vol. 3, p. 173.

6. Ibn al-Athir, *Al kamil fi al-tarikh* (Beirut: Dar al-Kutub al-ʿAlimiyya, 1987), vol. 8, p. 494. Ibn al-Athir died in year 630 of the Hejira.

7. *Algérie Actualité,* April 23–May 1, 1989.

8. Wahid al-Murakushi, *Al-muʿjib fi talkhis akhbar al-maghrib* (Casablanca: Kitab, 1987), p. 260. The author was writing in year 621 of the Hejira.

9. Algeria is one of the countries where this heightened violence against women is most spectacular; one can read about it almost any day in the newspapers.

10. The French and German publishers of my books always insist on having the word "harem" on the cover and a photo of a veiled woman. When I protest, they tell me that this makes it sell better, even if the contents of the book contradict this image. It is time to unveil women on the covers of books that sell in the West. Archaic attitudes don't exist on just one side of the Mediterranean.

11. *UNESCO Statistical Yearbook,* 1989, pp. 3251 (Iran), 3258 (Germany).

12. Farah Izari, article on the women's movement in Iran after the revolution, trans. from Persian into Arabic by Hala Shukr Allah and published in *Al-mar'a al jadida,* no. 2, July 1986, p. 25.

13. Figures for Pakistan are from *UNESCO Statistical Yearbook,* 1989; for Algeria see Nourredine Saadi, *Législation et condition feminine en Algérie: bilan des discriminations à l'égard des femmes,* report in the UNESCO Grand Programme 1, "Reflexions sur les problèmes mondiaux," September 1989, p. 47. An expanded version of this report entitled *Femme et loi en Algérie* was published in 1991 by Editions le Fennec (Casablanca) in its series Femmes Maghreb 2000.

14. *UNESCO Statistical Yearbook,* 1989.

15. Ibid.

16. See the memoirs of Huda Shaʿrawi, *Harem Years,* trans. and introduced by Margot Badran (New York: Feminist Press, 1987). The English edition was published by Virago Press in 1986.

17. Copies of papers presented by the Iranians Nayereh Tohidi, Val Mogadan, and Mohammed Tavakoli-Targhi, the Algerian Doraya Cherifati Merabtine, the Pakistani Khawar Mumtaz, the Nigerian Aicha Imam, and the Tunisian ʿAliya Bafoun can be requested from WIDER (World Institute for Development), a research center at the University of the United Nations in Helsinki. The proceedings of this conference, which was held in October 1990, should be published, and perhaps plans have been made to do so.

18. On Huda Shaʿrawi, see Badran (trans.), *Harem Years.* For an idea of the impressive Arab feminist movement at the beginning of the century see ʿUmar Kahhala, *Aʿlam al-nisaʾ al-ʿarabi wa al-Islam* (Famous Women of the Muslim and Arab Worlds) (Beirut: Muʾassasat al-Risala, 1982), 3 vols.

19. *UNESCO Statistical Yearbook,* 1989.

20. A recent study of the influence of women's writing is Khalida Saʿid, *Al-marʾa, al-taharrur, al-idbaʾ* (Woman, Liberation, Creation) (Casablanca: Editions le Fennec, 1991).

21. Some works by these writers have been published in English translation; see, for example, Hanane El-Cheikh, *The Story of Zahra* (London: Quartet Books, 1980); and Liana Badr, *A Compass for the Sunflower* (London: Women's Press, 1989). The address of the journal *Shahrazad* is 56 Griva Dhigeni Street, Limassol, Cyprus.

22. Kahhala, *Aʿlam al-nisaʾ.*

23. The Moroccan historian ʿAbd al-Hadi Tazi, in *Femmes célèbres de l'occident musulman* (Casablanca: Editions le Fennec, 1991), shows that the number of educated women held steady even in North Africa until the nineteenth century, when it steadily declined, compared to what it had been in Muslim Andalusia, for example, in the twelfth, thirteenth, and fourteenth centuries.

24. Proxy voting, which was strongly contested by Algerian women on the eve of the legislative elections in December 1991, was reconsidered, and husbands are now allowed to vote on behalf of their wives only in exceptional cases.

25. *UNESCO Statistical Yearbook,* 1988.

26. Ouahes, *Science et technology,* p. 19.

27. The outcry against mixing of the sexes cannot be understood if demographic changes are minimized, especially the trend toward later marriages, which, resulting from a combination of factors such as access to education, the decline of the extended family (requiring more people to earn their own living), the economic crisis, and unemployment, leaves single young men and women believers without a "fortress." Studies on marriage, especially recent demographic investigations, show that age at marriage is rising sharply in most countries of the Muslim world; see, for example, M. Chanine, *Women of the World: The Near East and North Africa* (Washington, D.C.: USAID, 1985). Whereas most women in Arab countries used to marry before the age of twenty, today not only are the majority of girls between the ages of fifteen and nineteen not married (93 percent in Tunisia, 86 percent in Lebanon, 72 percent in Syria, 70 percent in Morocco), but many between the ages of

twenty-five and twenty-nine are still single as well. A quarter of Lebanese single women fall in the latter age group; the proportion is 17 percent for Tunisia, 14 percent for Egypt, and 13 percent for Iraq. The same pattern can be found among men. In Egypt, for example, where a few decades ago men got married as early as possible, 43 percent of single men are now between twenty-five and twenty-nine years old, and 17 percent between thirty and thirty-four. In Tunisia 49 percent of single men are between twenty-five and twenty-nine years of age, and 16 percent between thirty and thirty-four; in Lebanon more than half the single men are between twenty-five and twenty-nine, and a quarter between thirty and thirty-four. Moroccan statisticians, who are usually as phlegmatic as any Englishman, speak in terms of catastrophe when they look at figures on the delay of marriage; see *Situation démographique régionale au Maroc* (Rabat: Centre d'Etudes et de Recherches Démographiques, Ministère du Plan, 1988), pp. 138ff.

28. George Corm, *Le Proche Orient éclaté* (Paris: Gallimard, 1991).
29. D. Nur 'Abdallah, *Al-petrole wa al-akhlaq* (Oil and Values) (N.P.: Editions Dar Doha, 1990); see especially the chapter "*Al-mar'a fi al-mujtama' al-petroli*" ("Woman in the Oil Society").
30. *Mémento Défense-Désarmement 1989* (Brussels: Groupe de Recherche et d'Information sur la Paix, 1989), pp. 183ff.
31. Ibid., p. 190.
32. Ibid.
33. Julia Kristeva, *Etrangers à nous-mêmes* (Paris: Gallimard, 1988).

CONCLUSION THE SIMORGH IS US!

1. Farid Ud-Din Attar, *The Conference of the Birds* (Harmondsworth, Eng.: Penguin, 1984), p. 219.
2. Ibid.
3. Ibid., pp. 219–20.

Index